Backtracking

Backtracking

Poems by

Dave Oliphant

T 93800

HOST PUBLICATIONS, INC.
AUSTIN, TEXAS

Layout and design: Joe Bratcher III
Cover design: Mary Lou Williams

Library of Congress Catalog Number: 2003116476
ISBN: 0-924047-24-0 (Hardcover)
ISBN:0-924047-25-9 (Trade Paper)

First Edition

Acknowledgments

Concho River Review for "A Texas Version of Crèvecoeur"

Inheritance of Light, edited by Ray González (University of North Texas Press) for "A Bullfight on Color TV" and "Rice"

Is This Forever, or What? Poems and Paintings from Texas, edited by Naomi Shihab Nye (Greenwillow Books) for "At the Surplus Supply"

Na.to.n Review for "Pulling Weeds for Princess Di"

Poesía y calle for "Constitutional"

RE: Arts & Letters for "Murphey's Law"

RiverSedge for "Ironing at the Colegio Mayor 'Mara'"

Roundup: An Anthology of Texas Poets, From 1973 to 1998 (Prickly Pear Press) for "María's Radio"

Seems for "María's Dresses," "María's Kieffer Pears," "María's Maine Coon Cat," "María's Meals," and "María's Sewing Machine"

Southwestern American Literature for "Extra Virgin" and "Tears"

The Texas Observer for "James White Bear Cody (1945-2002)"

Contents

España

from María's Poems

from **Backtracking**

Starting Over

Poets Teachers & a Librarian

España

An Occasional Ode

teachers of a second tongue
have come to Spain for '92
to this land brought change
to the map & language too

whole lives as well
those of others
for better or worse
only they can tell

but these for certain
would count the wealth
of a blend of words
mosarabic to Salamancan

to catch them have listened close
to the Madrilenian lips
of professors Olga & Piedad
they on tours the patient guides

steering where & how to partake of
monastery aqueduct & synagogue
to drink in stained-glass light
arts of ribbed dome & flying buttress

delivering their learned lectures
on Goya   El Greco   Velásquez
Picasso   Sorolla   El Escorial
their enthusiasm ever contagious

their deep delightful insights
filling these foreign ears & minds
with the colors shapes & lines
of a beauty & truth Hispanic style

by night turning Columbuses under sail
on three dorm-ships: Empresa Pública   Mara   Isabel
theirs a discovery route in reverse
travels them towards centuries of treasures

new worlds of custom & phrase
a vocabulary untasted before
in uttering each delicious place
in stuttering it out to savor

to relive the ancient look & feel
of cathedral castle or a city's fame
Segovia   Toledo   Cuenca   Seville
revisited now in repeating each name

but how to return the favor
can only hope to half-pronounce
the lilt of *vale vale* from every side
soon for students uneager to learn

those back home will be exposed
to Andalucía through print & slide
cards & posters from El Prado & Casón
zarzuelas heard & the Sevillana tried

their thanks extended to all of these
Guillermo   Irina   Begoña   Adela
Teresa   Juan   Leticia   Luis
Carmen   Blanca   Paloma Varela

& despite it all to conquistadors
braved   enslaved   & saved
traded   degraded   & remade
till in the end they at last created

a Rubén Darío   Vallejo   & Borges
a Mistral   Neruda   Lihn   & Paz
a Carpentier   & García Márquez
a Parra   Sábato   Puig   & Cortázar

4

theirs a linguistics richer than gold
the highest grade of an American ore
valued with Cervantes   Unamuno   & Lorca's
for any & every "materials" course

participants in the Quinto Centenario
they'll long gaze backwards & forwards
recall the magic date of his sighting land
brought them a subject to understand

if never fully to master
yet to know with love & respect
to impart with passion & pleasure
& in gratitude to Ortega y Gasset

Ironing at the Colegio Mayor "Mara"

with a hiss of the steam
& a clank of the iron   bare-
footed winter to pennant race
she would press them all again
those oxford button-downs with
short or each year longer sleeves

& while the hot slick metal
went sliding upon & smoothing
the sprinkled cloth   she'd listen
to her Dodgers field & bat around
removing once more the wrinkles
with a proud & tender touch

then taught this menial task
to lazy brothers college-bound
would have   she said   no money
for laundry bills as did those frats
yet her younger pledged & back at home
brought his dirty whites with monograms

never minded not she no not at all
washed them summer spring & fall
so affectionate his way with her
so full of kidding & forever wore
his impish grin those years before
that fatal crash had carried him off

elder & yet less willing or able
to say how much it always meant
in imitation then half showed it
in humid Austin so long ago
a shirt for work each morning
& now here again in hot Madrid

following still in all her steps
collars first & then the yokes
backs fronts & between the buttons
the pockets & last each sleeve & cuff
a pattern for every memory of
her dressing sons with highest hopes

a belated poem to express
her steam iron's warm caress
a distillation as of water poured
as she bent above that creaking board
to keep her boys handsome & clean
pulling still for that special team

Constitutional

as acacia seeds litter the tables
with a snow of life instead of cold
blown by this summer's evening breeze
this couple's come to promenade
up & down on these granite tiles

back & forth between the drinkers
the noise & noxious traffic fumes
here at the open-air Kiosco Parque
as cars & circulating buses pass along
each side of Queen Victoria Boulevard

reminds how Carlos called María's mother
"la reina madre"   in every way so tall & stately
to have been in stature so very short
while the man on their nightly stroll
looks so dour & self-assured

pompous really   not saying a word
to the wife holds onto his mechanical arm
bowlegged & struggling to keep his pace
in her ratty black-&-white ill-fitting dress
her worn & run-over slip-on wedges

think again of Gala so sophisticated
her carriage erect her clothes immaculate
taking her constitutional for deeper breaths
exemplary through all those difficult days
never to impress nor to appear superior

endured without complaint his wanton behavior
to die with a smile on her dignified face
a mother-in-law countered the comedians' jokes
her head held high though her heart half-broken
by a husband never valued his dearest treasure

by a daughter's damaged son unattended in time
when the indifferent obstetrician arrived too late
Gala missed by the fortunate few who knew her well
& without knowing it the kin who never will
may yet through flesh & blood inherit her sovereign way

Civil War

born the day it began
but three years later
in the one it ended

nothing to do with it really
though feel its bombs all falling now
inside this Anglo-Saxon brain

standing here before*Guernica*
with every face upturned in horror
as the horse by Picasso's art

stabs deeply with its dagger tongue
until can't help but hear it again
the joke about a Chilean who

on arriving was asked which side he was on
replied right away it didn't matter
since he had only come

to kill some Spaniards
it was religious difference drove a Puritan lot
to Plymouth Rock where they took it out

on the Iroquois & Narragansett
further south another conflict started over
States' Rights or so the Rebels swore

in Chile was undeclared
once three candidates split the vote
though still it's the same old story

with fathers opposing sons
brothers against brothers the way it was
with the two Machados

Manuel penning paeans to Franco
Antonio pitching with the Republican camp
in the '70s Paco Castaño pitted against

his & his brothers' Fascist folks
their mother's orders on Sunday mornings
to bring their colored ribbons home

would prove they had attended mass
knew which saint   had heard the homily
has told in poems of that oppressive past

now retraces it down his Salamancan steps
through narrow streets where Unamuno
Don Juan & Cervantes left immortal marks

not far from Lazarillo's lovely Tormes
the *pícaro*'s river mirrors majestic spires
a stone's throw from this ritual site

of bulls' throats slit in sacrifice
for a writing of doctoral students' names in blood
those passed their exams going out one door

to have bestowed that sacred honor
those failed made to stoop through a shorter
to face a crowd & be pelted with stones

Marga's later only painted on
in a harmless shade of red
not far from the National Archives

houses documents on their hated war
next door to another church or bar
nearly every entrance one or the other

within walking distance of Plaza Mayor
Bar Casanova   Catedral San Esteban
where Columbus found support

for his voyage to all the unlooked for
Catedral San Juan Bautista   Bar El Bardo
or Cafe-Bar Rua where that glorious day

Paco & his Marga would meet at last
just after she'd taught her literature class
not long after her lover had taken his life

Paco's own best friend who ended it all
torn apart by the forces struggle within
while these have survived to disagree

he her poet & she his critic
contraries drawn into   engaged in
their own state of peaceful siege

Fifty

just another round number yet half the way
to that magic hardly expected century mark
few reach some if they do unaware of the day
others having long before preferred the dark

now turn this age in Spain a homesick Texan
have seen in Segovia from circa a hundred B.C.
its aqueduct arches erected with unattached stone
a bridge of cut gray blocks nearly spans the city

still carries water from Eresma & Clamores far below
the Alcázar inaccessible at the edge of cliffs
a Disneyland castle complete with towers & moat
Isabel la Católica's sand clock of merely forty minutes

the length of time she would allow her kneeling subjects
"appeal tomorrow for permission to continue your sentence"
while all those Roman Arabian & Christian architects
built to last beyond this or any such human limits

A Bullfight on Color TV

have never been
nor would ever want to be
in this or any such arena

but stand here now transfixed
as natives pass along this street
have known it all before

are undisturbed it seems
makes one wonder the more
as they pause & stare

to compare the prices
of this store's imported sets
bearing signs declare a bargain

"reduced" as he will be
to his bloody knees
but only now emerges

with a chartreuse ribbon
fluttering from
his hump beginning to

bleed
as the picadors
tease & run for cover

safe behind
their protective wall
while he

slides in the circle of sand
bangs against the barrier
stuck now with

another ribboned stick
looking more man than beast
wearing his heart

upon his sleeve
as the toreador takes
his short effeminate steps

decked in sequins
& gold brocade
his thighs in tights a vivid pink

his white shirt
like a ruffled blouse
his shoes like those of ballerinas

with on his lips
a lighter shade of pink
as he holds his bright red cape

to hide the blade
all this somehow meant
to represent

one tormented
by the woman
of his fondest

dreams
but it couldn't be
it must say

something else
appears but the cruelest
flirting

for a crowd approves
when the victim sinks
to receive the

final sword
turn & leave
shamed by having looked

& by the torment of
all those have come
expecting love

Rice

from the bus's last & highest stop
have descended by Cuenca's cobbled streets
on the slick & treacherous slope of Anguish
to the hermitage of the Virgin of Grief

to find in her lap a crucified Christ
a grown man bruised & bleeding
held as if a babe in her arms
this city's patroness in black & gold

while a priest offers up the final prayer
& ends the mass with a sign of the Cross
standing just outside the open doors
am taken by the art of such figures within

till once again the past catches up
on spying between the shining stones
rice against their browns & grays
returns the happiness of that distant day

of her photo album retains it all
her beaming face among relations & friends
the plastic sack with the grains they threw
then nailed thorned speared & cruelly scorned

wounded & sliding on this ceramic religious scene
with her not here to protect & bless
off there miles away an ocean & more
when a grown man longs & needs to be

held to her holy mothering breast
wearing the black of mourning the Inca's gold
or better undressed for these alone
these adoring eyes agonizing till the close of death

17

from **María's Poems**

María's Albums

record the story of two lives together
fated to join though of distant cultures
of children half Texan arrived thereafter
of her Chilean relatives had gone before

recount one another's contrasting tones
her soft & warm come over from Spain
this harsh & blunt from a Saxon brogue
combined in binders & in cotton clothed

patterned prints with spines embroidered
each beginning & ending with a January
a tracing of the years from that 28th day
& its celebration of another anniversary

the flowers given & the books inscribed
the dinner out & the movie remembered
the cozy smokehouse had stayed the night
a gift of the kids saved quarters & dimes

the deaths of loved ones the heaviest loss
appearing on pages with pictures recall
Gala's knitting needles would dip & cross
on a last visit her customary evening walk

the pain remaining from a pet still missed
all the places lived she would never choose
though treasures in each a first word said
a quiet or trying moment she mustn't lose

these she's determined she must preserve
but despairs she will find the time it takes
to select from the slides those best return
the son or the daughter at that special age

the hours required for the writing by hand
or the drawings done with no photos found
stolen when the family had moved by train
a box emptied of each useless priceless scene

recollections jotted down & elementary tales
"I'm sick & tired" Miss Foy had told a class
how fit them in between her fixing the meals
doing laundry & the endless dishes to wash

faced with the ironing after her library work
not a minute left to assemble every souvenir
her teenage violinist in Amadeus's Salzburg
her ballerina danced in an annual Nutcracker

her morning job & then the cooking awaiting
beds to weed to water again without any rain
the others to make & the dusting & mopping
sox to darn a sink & tub need scrubbing clean

yet her colorful volumes nearly fill the case
scrapbooks spanning three decades & more
in her unadorned prose with its natural grace
narrated in a language some have rated poor

though rich to those who have read her words
been blessed by the annals of her selflessness
the sorrow & humor she so sedulously collects
crammed in the space her single closet affords

María's Ark

did it come from Goodwill
or another garage sale in the
subdivision of Anderson Mill

on Public TV the panel Bill
Moyers gathered for *Genesis*
argued whether it meant a cruel

God who could even kill
His own creation not of course
Noah & his motley crew

the only family on the block
would follow His rules
as when He said to build it

& Noah did
stocking it up
though the neighbors jeered

to him his God so good
that any not doing His will
was in his Middle English *wood*

but even in the surviving
Mystery play
his wife would not leap on

unless her gossips everyone
could all come too
until at last her son

had to drag her aboard
with camels polecats & swine
for the forty days of manure

here the animals are flat
cut out surely on an assembly line
painted dark gray or brown

facing in profile all in pairs
elephants giraffes lions & sheep
& how did the latter behave

how ever did the former fit
all now seeming to move
toward these miniature steps

at rest on the fireplace mantel
up against the hull of this ship
its roofed house set in the middle

to be loaded with symbols
from that biblical tale
its dove of love

its olive of peace
its rainbow sign of
an end to revenge

but just as much
the simple design
of two of each

male & female
climbing on together
knowing her

this must have been
what she had in mind
when she spotted & had to have

her bargain buy

María's Birds

it isn't that the doves jays cardinals or
wrens belong to her
but the feeders & the green plastic bath
she's placed outside this window
bring them here whenever they please
to peck at her store-bought sunflower seeds

to dip their beaks or splash their wings
no walls of wire to keep them in
coming & going by their own routine
as always at suppertime they seem to arrive
first one pink-footed dove then six or seven
flapping & maneuvering under the arbor's vines

the grape leaves shading their seeds & water
as they alight on the larger redwood roof
then hop down onto its platform holds
a box made out of cedar
heaped full with black or empty hulls
the latter if

she hasn't replenished their daily supply
their breasts too big to land or fit upon
the tiny wooden porches
of the smaller closed-in type
with its see-through panes
on two of its four rectangular sides

only the chickadees or titmice reach
to the seeds drop through
an opening beneath the glass
says she'll buy a book will identify
those whose names she doesn't know
though always they're recognized by

25

their crests & slightly reddish bands
watches each evening with delight
while she's eating her vegan meal
agreeing with Lindbergh who late in life
declared if he had to choose between
the planes he flew

his famous Spirit of St. Louis &
the many models he'd flown in since
would rather have her feathered friends
though how would she visit her people in Chile
of course the neighbors' cats prefer them too
over bags or cans of kitty food

tries shooing them away when they lie in wait
but those will come as free as birds
leaping the fence & over potted plants
to leave in the shrubbery a span of wings
of the taunting mocker who protected the nest
by dive bombing & strutting too close

each morning he would sing out front
from the mildew-resistant white crape myrtle
with his stream of unrepeated tones & rhythms
while those caught on coming to bathe or feed
those have bothered her so much more
feels deeply her love has done them in

yet every regret remains outweighed
by a need to catch their unfathomable flight
this & their colors & their nervous twitches
drawn by this artist of the airways
with kernels & a summer drink to a death-
defying performance in her backyard scene

María's Birthmark

on her upper arm the right outer
the skin's stained slightly darker
which even to the naked eye reveals
a mainland with archipelagic isles

or a planet surrounded by satellites
on lying near enough each night
& looking closer can even observe
a tumbling of sand-colored surf

on a beach invites exploring kisses
from there to press her warm soft lips
cover a lower row of crooked teeth
another "fault" she finds would ever keep

then reach to touch uneven toes
rub what to her's an outsized nose
nibble the lobes of dwarf-like ears
caress closed eyes have known few tears
except when Gala Sapo or Mushto died

stroke full-bodied hair now tinted to hide
where silver has sprung among brunettes
or yanked out   yet happily nothing corrects
nor needs to such "flawed" topographic features
exterior to a comely inscape no surface pictures

María's Clock

tells of a distant time
though close as all
her loved ones here

& though muffled after
she had it cleaned
its chime still rings

upon the hour
& at the half
to bring them back

long summer nights in Chile
in her country's "little north"
of how with supper over

Aguirre would make them sit
cousins all so dying
to hide 'n' seek outside

but would have to hear
his reading of
La Chimba's week-old news

word by word
those facts & figures
only now are adding up

here in this Texas home
kept current still
by a childhood mind

never behind those
happy happy times
more happy with

each pendulum swing
each tick & tock returns
the way they squirmed

in hardwood seats
their giggling together
when Gala would give her girls

a look so disapproved
she dutiful & intent upon
every dated notice he'd read

now hears it clearly again
can see it all unchanged
as in the patient shape

these roman numerals take
this brass-rimmed cracked
white porcelain face

passed over by a short
& longer hand
recount for her

that ageless day
page by
wondrous page

María's Dresses

no matter their price or how they've looked
found hanging on dismal bargain-store racks
stacked for sale in a stranger's garage or yard
in the end all alike have been transformed

not alone by laundering & changing a hem
by adding a bow or redoing a gaudy collar
by letting the waist out or by taking it in
but by covering clinging & softly conforming

like the simple white of that wedding day
made from her own drawing by her Tía Pepa
only showed her bare tanned arms between
the short sleeves & gloves of cotton netting

silk organdy to the throat & down to the floor
trimmed with a velvet sash of peaches pink
laced ruffle over tips of delicate slippered feet
hair held by a ribbon a veil couldn't wait to lift

María's Genealogy

a lapsed Catholic herself
rather like her mother
who never went to mass
but never failed to pray

yet if unanswered right away
quickly appealed to another saint
though at least her younger daughter
has attended on the two big dates

that winter birth & springtime death
though instead of the Roman church
has kidded how she may convert
to the polygamous Latter-Day faith

smiles to remember in Chile
how all along her Pyramid street
neighbors would yell in warning
then close their shutters & doors

at the identical coming of
a white-shirted necktied pair
one short one tall traveling together
to offer each year in their

broken Spanish the origins of
that sacred Book of Mormon
though saddened now to recall
a young man murdered in Austin

had served his time by walking
each unfriendly belligerent block
to bring the news to every race
others sent farther to photograph

the records of married & deceased
in every out of the way diocese
Ovalle where on January 12th of '44
Gala was delivered of my pride & joy

her second child who prefers
dusty La Chimba to anywhere else
another unheard-of country place
her grandfather's in *el norte chico*

needed to know of its former life
ways her mother had had to go
what trains she took to school
in distant towns like Rengo

wanted as well to identify
those her line descended from
to find them had to drive
to their Family History Center

to order through Salt Lake City
handwritten archives on microfilm
to view in Texas the Chilean names
decipher the four centuries of entries

for reconstructing her Aguirre tree
all the wedded cousins & their issue
the generations on her maternal side
down to her own & her sister's too

tracing back to 1540 when out of Perú
Francisco most loyal captain to Valdívia
crossed with that conqueror the Atacama
second worst desert in all the world

born 1500 in Talavera de la Reina
he her first relation came to Chile
governor-defender of La Serena
against Drake & his buccaneers

marauders of her native coast
burning homes & inventories
kept accurate for every parish
her forebears born & buried

later made mayor of Santiago
capital city where she gave consent
for this traded her storied nation
where now she reads how at 69

in La Plata he lay imprisoned
three years awaiting delayed release
by order of the King would hear & respond
to news they'd dragged his faithful servant

before the Inquisition in Chuquisaca
marched in chains from Tucumán
back across the Andes & the Atacama
to be accused of heresy in word & deed

ninety crimes against religion
among them how not hearing mass
could bring no harm to those he said
in hearts commend their souls to God

how Plato could equal in thought
the gospel according to the Evangel John
how excommunication frightened little men
not him who never feared dishonest priests

would eat not fish but meat on Fridays
on holidays had his Indians work the fields
declared heaven & earth could pass away
but not the truth he was sworn to say

then bareheaded forced to confess his errors
by a bishop & viceroy both so covetous
the authority Philip II vested in him
those at last having convinced the throne

the Americas should have a Tribunal sit
whose accusations continued until '76
when he returned to his fruits & flowers
orchards & gardens won in Araucanian wars

after 40 years & just before his end at 81
from New Spain writing his final lines
declaring he'd faithfully served his sire
along with chattel & his own offspring

spending 300 thousand of his personal pesos
losing brother sons son-in-law & nephews
discovering subduing & settling a kingdom
in the name of his highness whose hands & feet

his vassal kissed from the blue Pacific
her long thin land she now revisits
by virtue of the words of that conquistador
& through those trust in the mystic power

of a prayer can save from eternal death
all those ancestors who ever lived
before that sacred revelation
of their founder Joseph Smith

María's Hands

hers are nothing like the ones in ec-
clesiastical portraits El Greco made
that of a cardinal in cap cape & lace
rendered with thin elongated fingers
beringed & extended on rich red cloth
hers though short aren't stubby at all
of a feminine form yet softly strong
her delicate nails with quarter moons
uncovered with polish or silver glitter
never rise nor set but shine the same
through whatsoever they move or lift
pencils & pens copybooks & spirits
as they wash lettuce or a toilet bowl
pots & pans peel potatoes or carrots
with her right second digit slightly bent
from its being caught in a bicycle chain
its larger joint bearing a permanent scar
the pinky showing a sympathetic bend
tender at times from her fibromyalgia
& on the left a simple wedding band
unadorned gold from a Chilean store
owned by the family of a Jewish friend
her best certainly no sparkling diamond
at another shop at the Square of Arms
had the accepted name engraved inside
only once took it off as a protest sign
on finding its mate had been removed
from pain when worn in a round of golf
at school never took any typing lessons
though at a keyboard so accurate & quick
her indices doing as much as any two can
with gloves on will dig in the hardest earth
o such comfort comes of feeling them bare
while walking or sitting or too sore to hold
just having them laid on to minister & heal

María's *hermana*

known as Coneja
from her rabbit-like
two front teeth

pushes against them
her index finger as she muses
& makes connections

though on one occasion
called Sapita
from her frog-like

habit of staring
of eavesdropping
on whatever the others

have had to say
discerning in every way
always her taste

discriminating
decorating her home
made cozy with

her own creations
framing them too
& as one artist friend

declared after years & years
of classroom training
lessons in drawing

sculpting & painting
self-taught Cony
can do it all

& all so natural
takes any material
& selects a shade

designs & shapes
cuts & pastes
clips out a collage

each gift she gives
with a native motif
a desk or hope chest with

her drawing of
a fuchsia magellanica from
Chile's southern tip

each deep
red pistil
precisely brushed

as a botanist would
stamen anther filament
exquisitely done

or chooses a rejected
remnant to become
far more than

it had ever been
she a college dropout
never finished her degree

meant to be a teacher
of English as a second
language as Gala was

who taught for 30 years
but Cony too painfully shy
preferred being housekeeper

a cook for her mother
as she prepared her classes
marking the endless exams

& for María who rode
crammed on buses
taking them late

to her library work
of stamping & repairing
the battered books

arriving home to
nutritious dishes
clean linen & spotless floors

a warmth of walls with
Cony's fresh surprising sketches
ever in season

soothing tones for
summer & spring
in winter vivid

in autumn subdued
grateful to her though even so
the two could always disagree

over politics or a father
whom Cony adored
while María knew

so long before
he'd been untrue
to their beloved mother

at 14 even
had written to him
when he'd left for Rio

to receive the prize
the one he'd won
for a cover design

in a contest held by
a Brazilian firm
said We're happier

whenever you're gone
Please do not return
Talent's no excuse

for abusive treatment
her words so convincing
he never came home

poor Cony
could never forgive
María's letter

kept her daddy away
never to see him
ever again

dead of cancer
at last report
his radio show

his party jokes
his award-winning story
printed by Zig-Zag

that leading press
even María conceding
his sense of humor

his ingenuity
his artistic bent
inherited by Cony

& by Darío too
while María takes after
Gala more

their mother's level head
her common sense
though she too got his wit

but hers
a happy disposition
where Cony received

her father's temper
by turns loving
or a volcanic eruption

& his charming gift as well
for summing up with a bon
mot friend or foe

his names for those
a perfect fit
such cunning fun

made of one & all
though never able
to take it himself

while Cony's comic side
is never public
her satirical touch

reserved alone for
the family at home
composes for gatherings

her questionnaires
clever & handwritten upon
folded slips of paper

to be answered
by those whose
every habit

every eccentric trait
she uncannily knows
her little barbed queries

even bring to bull's-eyes
of her darling targets
laughter's tears

her house filled
with mates of
sons & daughter

all feeling at ease
& confiding in
this adopted aunt

who after they've studied
late or drunk
too much

will feed them first
then prepare their pallets
her husband quietly

footing the bill
his heritage another source
of sibling dissent

his Palestinian blood
running as if as much in her
as in their three offspring

counter to María's
own affection for
her Jewish friends

Edith & Gerard
who only missed
the holocaust from

his having taken
a job in Spain
married one year

then apart for a decade
a separation by Civil War
then reunited in the U.S.A.

& later in '64
would visit Chile
he working for NASA

said he'd heard a lecture
Einstein gave
admitted he hadn't

understood a thing
could still from memory
quote in German

from Goethe's *Faust*
write perfect Spanish
his wife reading far & wide

at the Institute
had met María who
checked out books to her

on every subject
then began to chat a bit
lunched together

hiked the Andes
with her second parents
a childless couple

had taken her in
though Cony & the others
would find it wrong

complained was wasting
every weekend with
such an elderly pair

instead of dating
would remind her again
of her increasing age

was 22 & needed
to be out & about
securing a man

differing in this
& ever since on the issue
of Arab & Jew

yet knowing well one another's view
will let it alone
María rather recalling

how much she hated
when she had to wear
Cony's hand-me-downs

school uniforms stained
with ink she'd drip
skirts smeared & yellowed

with avocado or quince
these marking
a difference between

one neat & orderly
the other given
to art's original

sloppy vision
& even though
so unalike

forever close
meanwhile the partial
Texas observer

tries his best
to take no side
though how can he help

but go along
with the one
he chose &

yet has forever felt
doubly blessed
being from the first

made welcome by
this sister-in-law
who knew so well

courtship would mean
a continent between
waiting long for a letter

or the phone to ring

María's Kieffer Pears

hard & huge & half-hidden
among the thick green leaves
of smooth-skinned gray-brown limbs
have shot up tall as the angled roof

are reached by a trick she's taught
of a two-by-four-inch board
eaten at the edge from being before
stuck on its side & propped by stones

to keep the earth in her salvia bed
of tying to either end a rusted can
of twisting until have heard a snap
& they drop inside with a gentle clunk

then ease them down & lift them out
as mosquitoes swarm at shoes & cuffs
as fruit already fallen from wind & rain
draws bees by a rich aromatic ferment

placed on a dish in the dining room
they call for an artist's oil & brush
to catch their glow of reddish-pink
freckled blush against the yellow-green

each stiff & broken umbilical stem
atop the smaller of graceful swells
together shaped to a sensuous pair
though for most the meat's too tough

unsold in stores unworth the trouble
more often than not are left to rot
stuffed beneath a Depression mattress
softened somewhat as the indigent slept

till blisters form on her fingertips
will peal & slice & dig out knots
then simmer with sugar & cinnamon
their white flesh to a burnished tan

from the steam every room is redolent
with their clean & wholesome fragrance
afterwards cooled & served as dessert
shared with friends know how to tell

the taste & tenderness her stewing gave
her recipe began with backyard grown
the brightness of their earliest blooms
filled her tree with a flowering of light

survived the last cold spell in April
then cast below its snow-white shadow
gone from where each globe stayed on
ballooning full & firm the summer long

pecked at by flights of passing birds
until the time for bringing them down
to hand them over to her loving touch
works such wonders with fire & water

María's Maine Coon Cat

after his whiskered face
tufted cheeks striped legs
& perfectly rounded paws

appeared sitting upon
her backyard cedar bench
his huge yellow eyes

staring in hope & fear
she yearned to know
the life he lived before

then invented for him
an abusive history
of being left outside

in lightning & thunderstorm
can lower him still
as the sight of a

broom or stranger
will flatten his fluffy tail
make him growl &

run for cover under
dresser couch or bed
arrived unsexed & bedraggled

& against every objection
her Siamese had been
trouble enough

she coaxed him in
when taking over
her heart & home

his long sharp claws
ruined the new front door
& though her skin unmarked

kills her instead with
his golden belly spread
protected on windowsills

by crape myrtle & abelia
photinia & bridal wreath
she thrilled by the primal beast

shows through as he stalks
in among the rosemary
Mexican oregano salvia & mint

leave his mottled coat
matted & scented with
spent blooms removed

as she brushes pets & kisses
whispering into his ear
how he's her sweetie pie

the most beautiful creature
in the whole wide world
who made it miraculously

from New England here
her unlooked-for gift
has brought such treasure

as no lottery she says
no fame nor glory
could ever

which goes as well for her
who accepted that
awkward invitation to

a first date can never forget
since lucky as he
with his hope & fear

it has meant
being let in
to all of this

María's Meals

ill in Chile
had yet to wed
she telephoned by
the landlady said

was deathly afraid
whatever it was
would surely spread
had other boarders

she had to think of
so fetched by cab
hurried to her home
gotten into her bed

so sick it seemed
the most natural thing
when tucked between
her clean white sheets

brought a steaming bowl
of consomé
noodles boiled & served
with salt & oil

apples stewed
manzanilla tea
have kept up strength
forever since

or was it sleeping
where Beauty slept
on her pillow where
she lay her head

made whole again
by the nourishment of
her dishes prepared
day by day

cured most from being
so close can savor
the delicacy
of all her care

María's Memo

made the administrators pee in their pants
sent them scurrying to find that Chapter 9
with the very section paragraph & line
forbid lobbying legislators on university time

& while the mice-men kept their profiles low
weathering the controversy well out of sight
she carried it to those high-ups of might makes right
waging for all classified staff the glorious losing fight

María's Metempsychosis

not to hear the rude remarks she so resents
says next time around will marry an orphan
be spared those in-laws must always hint
how awfully wrong she has raised her kids

even better will return in an animal's skin
of dog or cat eats & sleeps for half the day
barks or scratches at the door to be let in
to shrieks of delight   petted watered & fed

in dishes will never wash dry nor ever refill
yet most gives pause when she simply declares
will come back male & be done once & for all
with lumps in the breast   a fibrous uterus

& what will that leave but a choice between
gay or female   & how is that going to feel
whatever shape shade or gender she takes
paired with her again would be nirvana still

María's Miracles

she performs them day or night
as when she gives the cat a kiss
on its furry bluepoint face
then lets it stretch & softly knead

with paws against her Chilean cheek
when husband & kids all hoot & hiss
yet believe in this miraculous sight
permitted even the unworthy witness

María's Radio

keeps her company & up to date
entertaining her as she cooks & bakes
marathons in advance of weekly meals
each delicious dish will nourish & fill
the curried chicken over a bed of rice
Texmati or jasmine with an onion slice
first skinned deboned & boiled to a froth
to make the base for a tasty natural broth
for homemade soups of her vegetable mix
or of spinach alone so healthful & iron rich

her favorites the local Scots announcer-singer
Ed Miller on "Folkways" & Garrison Keillor's
"Prairie Home Companion" Terry Gross too
with her knowns & unknowns to interview
on "Fresh Air" & "Car Talk's" philosophical
grease-monkey brothers who at every call
yuk it up as they dispense advice on muff-
ler ignition switch hydraulic lift along with love
together on NPR with "All Things Considered"
whiling away the only hours ever hear her dread
those spent starching & pressing blouses & shirts
will catch but bits & pieces yet it always irks
on just passing through to the "reading room"
where only jazz & classics would ever presume
not so much that Scotch-Gaelic pathetic whine
but rather Paul Ray's program of "Twine Time"

worse than Keillor's satirical lives of cowboys
horse-backed megabites in woe-begone voice
for it's Ray returns to mind her teenage years
*Sixteen Candles The Great Pretender Tears
on My Pillow Twilight Time* or *Party Doll*
when on slow numbers she will still recall

how Jaime invited her great dancer bigger tease
with parents permitting no Gentile steadies
see her rocking in his arms around the clock
to *Itsy Bitsy Teenie Weenie Yellow Polka Dot*
Bikini It's My Party Little Darling Only You
till the green-eyed beast again breaks through
almost prefer at seventeen she *had* become
as she vowed she would a noiseless nun
no longer to judge a date by socks he wore
how well he could clutch or in soccer score

though in those days not there only later met
she already twenty-two & knew well was get-
ting a gringo stepped on toes & couldn't sing
couldn't stand his own forebears' Highland fling
a Texan given to the darkest of Irish moods
not half so smart nor clever as all those Jews
she's ever admired & yet will share the shows
that he may learn through her of trumpet solos
by Marvin "Hannibal" Peterson of Smithville
then ride in their son's Fairmont cherry mobile
to San Antone & hear together the live quartet's
performance with orchestra of *African Portraits*
insisting that he hurry out of the gloom & listen
to Billy Taylor analyze on "Morning Edition"
Strayhorn's *Lush Life* with its amazing changes
such progressive harmonies as she too arranges

María's Sewing Machine

is heavy enough
to have carried it
as far as she

would have given
most men a hernia
for certain me

she making it through
Santiago & Lima
on then to Miami

where at customs
on purpose
she chose

a Spanish-speaking
official with his
neck encased in foam

couldn't bend
to inspect her bul-
ging luggage con-

tained her treadle
her cast-iron heritage
with its top of warped

& cracking wood
not to be sold to
the highest bidder

wouldn't trade it in
for the latest Singer
with fancy attachments

she tied to this
by all her blood
her youth & childhood

am to her
as bobbin
to thread

together
come what may
will sing her

through every age
who can alter any cloth
hem or reupholster

slipcover & by her
sense of humor
leaves me in

stitches of love

María's Souvenir

her cane poles
from the Ely market
are short & thin
no good for fishing

but then she isn't much on sports
a soccer fan when younger
till she caught herself
yelling & screaming out of control

bought & carried them
onto the plane
for crossing them where
the Titanic didn't

for propping up in the yard
her flowers & plants
found them at a vendor's
with its Cathedral view

spared by Cromwell
who lived next door
the isle a dowry of Etheldreda
named for eels before

Dutchmen drained its fens
its famed Octagon-shaped
Lantern Tower its arch-
lined hall-like Nave

red & green depictions
so high the figures
barely seen
flying buttresses

impressive as those in Spain
less decorative though
angels hovering & far below
the bishops at rest

posed with hands on chests
& at their feet creatures
carved or sculpted
meaning God knows what

names in the chapel
like Allgood & Piggott
the first recalling in Altus
that Oklahoma boyhood friend

now a doctor the other an actor
played on Masterpiece Theatre
that unsavory role
in *Jewel in the Crown*

such history's the catch
though nothing perhaps
she intended these stems
mean more to her than

any civil or religious war
royal wedding gifts
naves angels bishops
niches of little worth

so many ravenous
elongated slimy fishes
no luxury liner nor raj can vie
with her hollow jointed sticks

María's Tambourine Man

having to hear his harmonica & guitar & smart-
assed voice day after day's not the worst part
nor watching in the bedroom as the little space
shrinks while his shrine fills with bootleg base-
ment tapes books like *Song & Dance Man III*
his Brit tour on video re-releases any new CD

nor is it having to hear her *Rolling Stone* read
on a fan dumpster-diving to recover cigarette
butts for DNA to clone Dylan once he's done
digging in trash for any song draft he rejected
listening to more sightings from bobolinkdotnet
or countless biblical allusions in "Highway 61"

rather it's having about the house a superstar
whose lyrics she's gotten by heart that is far
worse or in conversation drops some phrase
of his when labored lines dedicated to praise
her every feature still remain unmemorized
unattended unlike his concerts over apprized

by millions swoon yelling his precious name
throwing any item hoping he'll only touch it
toss it back miraculously with his autograph
yet even with all his followers & all his fame
he hasn't heard or put together how much it
means her humming "It Takes a Lot to Laugh"

how her "Slow Train Coming" lets out a sigh
& her "Man Gave Names to All the Animals"
whistled can change the times turn even blues
or "Desolation Row" from lowdown to high
had tried tuning him out swearing flat denials
it was worth the trouble could accept Jews

61

in classical & jazz even in Tin Pan Alley
but not one aping folksy Woodie Guthrie
every prejudice fallen on sweet deaf ears
she the best defender for a hopeless case
will win it by a look on her zealous face
by a music she's made of all these years

from **Backtracking**

1

not out of fear that a fork in the road
some turn not taken ended wrongly here
but rather to follow the twists of fate

& see if they are or if it's a matter of choice
to reckon the cost they thought it worth
when it didn't pan out the way they hoped

for it still seems right to remember them
who held to what their minds' eyes saw
though now it's not the same nor even close

far in fact from the dreams bequeathed
regretted half the time as misconceived
the other for having failed to measure up

in spite of all to trace back state by state
harder perhaps on a Texan with little use
for anything arriving from north or east

till swallowing pride head out for lands
some settled before they could receive
a welcome from these hills & plains

wonder why in Arkansas others failed to stay
where harvested fields of wheat & hay
wear a country boy's home-cut hair

forsaking the miracle of terraced rice
greened by irrigation though only after
could clear the brush & uproot trunks

once their plows had broken through
where the John Deeres now will stir up dust
the drivers safe in air-conditioned glassed-in cabs

yoked teams stumbling then on shining clods
car tires thumping here on hunks of littered tread
black as the backs of alligators in Cajun swamps

waded through to reach some higher ground
free of crowds at drive-ins another Day's Inn
a search rarely found nor did they think to seek

a viola's phrase a verse's measured line
looking more for an unstagnated stream
an uneroded unexhausted terrain

virgin soil for slaves to hoe for picking
the cotton crop until they'd drop
then lifted by beer & Memphis blues

but not there yet not even near
when a convoy of trucks in camouflage
khakied troops miles from Joplin's town

halt at a rest area erected by public funds
a muscled corporal peeling a pungent orange
while his fellow blacks line up to take their turns

not the relief seasick immigrants were searching for
after perilous passage through sacred burial grounds
down treacherous cliffs into raging creeks

breaking backs over plantings plagued by drought
to arrive at familiar billboards still proclaim
a self-same tasteless fast-food chain

despair of finding anything more or even a clue
why they'd risk it even as far as Little Rock
to eat from the sweat of another's brow

forsaking Georgia farms for Visa freedom
only to have an Ike send in the National Guard
for escorting integration up their high school steps

when soon enough franchises of Sears & Dillard's
would pave another tempting parking lot
issue disfranchising credit cards

then make it at last to the Mississippi
only to find it so low no barge can go
though Huck & Jim still raft & smoke

drift past each prejudice & deadly feud
unhurried on the same slightly undulant flow
that convict spends years in the shadow of

though unseen its subway rumble ever hears
bearing its constant flotsam of scum & twigs
washing away the Colonel's Belles Demoiselles

whirling & seething at his inherited banks
diminishing a grant gained by his bigamist genitor
its willowy bend rustling with miles of cane

the scheming son's mansion tipped over & sunk
his seven lovely daughters swept away & under
by the rising waters of its unfathomable flood

for Adelantado Hernando de Soto
a long wet kiss from his endless lover
as he sinks a solitary sperm to her hog-sized fish

source of the false charity of a Con Man's plot
of those silent hosannas with their liquid theme
now in early June running unmajestic & thin

with snowfall low in the whole Midwest
spring come & gone with no trace of rain
& is it then an omen for all the loss

the little to be recovered on trekking back
to revisit the faded glory of a river's past
this Great Sire reduced to barely a trickle

its envisioned new freights & far other ends
its towering smokestacks all so grand
a royalty billowing balls of steam & soot

giant triple-decker wedding cakes
boilers overheating then bursting in flame
deadly holes blown in giant hulls then buried hulks

till poking up with drought their skeletons reveal
from that Civil War the "Paul Jones" "Dot" & "Charm"
scuttled in retreat now archaeologists roping them off

in a race against mother nature swallowing again
scavengers sneaking around in search of gold
ripping off a relic the harness for mule or horse

a stack of dinnerware chipped & cracked
a bottle of antidote for ague or fever
a stern paddle hardly worth the wading

ankle-deep in slimy weeds
then a crowd gathering nearby at Handy Park
where facing Beale W.C. stands a statue

with behind him & to the right
a ring encircles an urchin with in his mouth a recorder
three guitarists a trumpeter a mechanical drummer

come to carry on a tradition of yellow dogs
of blind men singing on Depression corners
pilgrims to this Mecca to this training ground

for all-night sessions of the separate & unequaled
a Charlie Robinson discovering others' higher notes
were nothing to him his two octaves range enough

for reaching & holding any listener's heart & soul
who slugged corn whiskey & gambled till dawn
danced on the piano top to his own unrecorded song

grandsons & daughters tapping feet & clapping hands
keeping time as if this were where & what
the convoys & wagons were destined for

or was it Graceland & Elvis' grave
a gaudy show of bouquets & granite markers
photographs commemorating his patented shake

trim in his white suit red sash & Hawaiian lei
filmed on site in the Marquesas with palms asway
rowed between canoes on a banana-leaved stage

every native eye fixed on his slicked back hair
though no more cannibalistic than moviegoers
would eat him alive in his B-rated scene

all still hunting him with chants of Elvis Lives!
as if by rearranging the letters of his given name
could bring him back who killed him with worshipped fame

their bloated King of Rock 'n' Roll
fallen to drugs & alcohol the price each paid
any for the treasured autograph or Snappy photo

for silk thread sequin or a single strand
swooning as he crooned "Love Me Tender Love Me True"
oh something the dollar bills could never do

though to buy Golden Hits assured he'd never die
his voice forever revived on "Blue Suede Shoes"
escaping death's cold iron bars with "Jailhouse Rock"

at "Heartbreak Hotel" staying with him night after night
as on the cover of *Life* his daughter his look-alike
brings back every feature down to his feminine lips

speaking in her first exclusive interview
of the pills he took of the gift he gave
her own battery-powered golf cart at the age of four

so was it worth it after all
if this is where the picture ends
or is it then that each may choose

even Lisa remembering a father's good
& this by choice once she's understood
the legendary man whose face her own returns

each city offering a Presley or a Father of the Blues
or others whose stories though lesser known
deserve retelling like that Mississippi moan

punctuated by Lunceford's flaming brass
anchored by Jock Carruthers on baritone
the Trio belting out those corny lyrics none surpass

Muddy water in my shoes / I'm rockin' to the lowdown blues
I don't care it's muddy there / it's still my home
they live in ease & comfort there

I declare
my toes turn Dixieway
round & round the delta let me stay

as much for the shoals & bars espied
as for such depths sounded in all they sang
their cargo of fellowship & sacrifice

those pulled together to make it up
when the current aimed to sweep them down
but this gets ahead of a tale began at Fisk

only later would Jimmie move to Memphis
here where two barbers attended the annual convention
in that first Faulkner novel had ever read

here the pair taking a decent room
wonderfully cheap though hardly getting a single wink
with noises all night through adjoining walls

people climbing stairs & walking the halls
squeaking springs with half-pained half-soothed tones
each evening finding on their bed or floor

or draped in the bath on tub or commode
ladies' intimate underclothes
couldn't figure it out & never would

& though this first night's accommodations
superior to any in a Modern Library edition
may yet remain as stumped as a couple of yokels

but plan to continue where the map will lead
to the eastern beginning of Estevan's Texas plot
retracing steps to a view from Mt. Everett's crest

next stop the Fugitives' gathering spot

2

in her 80s Granny Polk would always say
"I'm going to see my boyfriend in Nashville Tennessee"
but first she'd have to fix her face

brush her dentures & do her nails
work into her girdle fasten snaps held up her hose
step into a pair of her highest heels

at her home on Western near the Country Club
would prepare those same predictable meals
celery sticks & black-eyed peas

mostly leftovers a dab of this a dab of that
a trait from Depression days when any scrap
left by boarders at breakfast she'd always save

cutting crusts from the lunches she'd pack
in black metal pails for those would find them
turned to bread pudding come suppertime

her birthday on Valentine's a dead giveaway
liked men & still had them on bended knee
she seated on a green bench in her beloved Saint Pete

but at 15 had married Mose back in '98
grandad 10 years her senior was done for by 59
in her witty words "the Oliphants die young"

in her family she the oldest sent at 13 to Murfreesboro
a country girl cared for a relative's brood of half-a-dozen
& forever swore "I'd rather be in jail with my back broken

than baby-sit a pack of kids" though even so
had six of her own the first two in Tennessee
the last four in Baird a junction just as barren as ever could be

but better for asthma grandaddy thought
though would never evade his recurrent TB
to him his honey had hung the moon

& proud too of Fannie Lil Carl Doll & Winnie
but most of all his Mosby Davis
the son to whom he gave both his southern names

died in '32 before his junior had gotten engaged
who yet would tell his dad he had found his mate
had never talked to mother yet knew they would wed

heir to his honest ways his mother's get-up & go
her comic commentary on any lazy crew including her own
accused them of "laying with the dry cows all night long"

a good-for-nothing she called "a walking miscarriage"
lambasted herself as well for bearing them all
"I should have slept with my face to the wall"

after Mose retired would move to Fort Worth
she selling ready-to-wear he coughing & fading away
she keeping cornbread & cabbage on the kitchen table

with a pink powder puff repainted her Oldsmobile
sent their elder son to A & M though it didn't take
saw the oldest marry an alcoholic with Hoerner Box

mercifully grandad gone before he knew the worst
their first son ending his days in the state asylum
their first daughter's son in & out of prison

what would Mose have thought not dying so soon
living to witness the toll taken by their Texas move
leaving his "Athens of the South" for tumble weeds

traded Vanderbilt for a desolate railhead east of Abilene
or was it just from turning to him her tender face
that Brother ended up nutty a grandson shot cocaine

had met & married here where two decades later
Tate & Ransom taught & Lunceford took his degree
but did Mose suspect it "'a nostril' through which the state

had long breathed the Northern air of free institutions'"
would he have ever imagined an ex-student's engines
set up in a Georgia Industrial School amazed even klansmen

or when asked where he learned such mechanical skills
could answer it came of studying a bit of ancient Greek
did Mose & Polk believe it all but a coat of paint

scratch it & beneath the surface a savage would stir
or their brain suture's closing prematurely the cause
of higher faculties inactive after age twelve to fourteen

not wanting to think it yet must in recalling that past
as General Fisk said for learning "the terrible lessons"
a wonder dad never used the "N" word nor saw them as beasts

when out near Liberty one in a pick-up ran into him
dad permitted the unlicensed old driver to "pay as you can"
& monthly like clockwork the postman delivered his five-dollar
                                                        bill

dad's faith so like George White's who trusted still
when even Fisk his commander at Chancellorsville
turned down a loan for keeping open that failing school

& to think it would bear his General's name
White hearing the words of Leviticus 25 loud & clear
"the trumpet of the jubilee shall sound throughout the land"

with scarce food enough for one more week
this untrained music director would take on tour
his newly emancipated Jubilee choir

his singers deep in debt yet donated even so
their proceeds from a recital in Ohio
to tragic victims of a Chicago fire

with no hotels willing to put them up
George would change their luck
instead of pop tunes had them do their slavery songs

spirituals expressive of their American lives
at the White House for Grant sang "Go Down Moses"
to be greeted there with appreciative applause

sang in E-flat "Battle Hymn of the Republic"
three half-steps higher than normal & with no burnt cork
in Europe the younger Johann Strauss waved his violin

as an electrified audience threw up their handkerchiefs
on hearing "He hath sounded forth the trumpet
. . . shall never call retreat"

Du Bois attending here then Harvard
where he found the teachers no better
said were only more widely known

& better paid though never so eager to feed
students hungering for a fruit so long forbidden
reading & writing to them such a holy mystery

while whoever taught was whipped & spit upon
down yes Church Street the Klan in defiant parade
as pupils on their way to class were openly stoned

those starved more for learning than even for food
would sell scrap metal old rusty handcuffs
just to buy the power of talismanic books

by World War I with 76 stars from Fiskites fallen
still the lynchings & brutality would go right on
3,000 accepting a newspaper invitation to watch one burn

& their music room in such sad repair
the wall paper flapping in winter's wind
as through the roof & walls the rain came in

for an instructor's feet & lap only heated bricks
& still they enrolled like the one had written "I beg to state
that I wants to be come a student at Fisk

and wants to Board where I will be warm"
little knowing the conditions so bad they turned all women
                                                    away
returning upperclassmen surviving summer on seven
                                            cents a day

& what became of White the pioneer whose troupe
Twain said he'd walk seven miles to hear
even the Kaiser's men hoping to learn from them

when they brought to Germany their sorrow & yearning
their finest tenor spitting up blood with inspiring song
before that in Scotland his wife succumbing to typhoid

one singer always ill one suffered a stroke
as they poured out "Nobody Knows the Trouble I See"
the untrained director prostrated with a hemorrhaging lung

& did Mose ever know of their Jubilee Hall
hear them sing "Steal Away" or "John Brown's Body"
would it have meant anything to him Tate translated Pindar

how could it to one only switched & shunted freight cars
who likely had no suspicion any direct descendant
would know of or even want to read "Blue Girls" by Ransom

or "Bells" for John Whiteside's long-dead daughter
how could that assignment from Robert Nossen
mean a thing to him who just wanted to be certain

the westbound train was still on time
checking his pocket watch the one engraved
with initials now of four generations

his only heirloom he handed down
no message no signature just the registrar's
& doctor's on a standard certificate where

the Bureau of Vital Statistics has recorded
principal cause coronary occlusion with
tuberculosis of kidney & lungs contributory

no autopsy performed no proof nothing to do but guess
he'd have had not the least interest in any quatrain
with "word" & "sward" its fine off-rhyme

but why is it so important to know if an immigrant son
of some ignorant poor-white Scottish clan
born a Southerner in a defeated unreconstructed land

might have given the time of day
to Tate's "Ode to the Confederate Dead"
bothered to agree with Lowell as to Allen's best

his marvellous "Swimmers" in terza rima
much less accepted indictment of lynching's strangest fruit
why even conceive a railroader could ever react

to his second son's coming to listen in fact
to Jimmie's two-beat swing with joy & love
when not even the Fugitives ever visited Fisk

to find & hear that future conductor's
Cotton Club Express
grandad's only line the Southern Pacific not one of Dante's

& yet there has to have been something way back here
to account for an offspring every time he'd hear
responding deeply to "Lunceford Special" & "Stratosphere"

or maybe owed it more to his mother's ear
she whose first name was Jimmie too
though her own taste running exclusively to

the saccharine sounds of that Champagne man
how ever explain how it came about
if not through blood how figure it out

maybe it's up ahead on another trail
one blazed by Boone or a Moses Austin
who said hundreds traveled not knowing for what

or whither except it was on to Kentucky

Starting Over

Another Hill Country Sunset

while clouds pile up in puffs
like white-powdered coiffured wigs
in eighteenth-century drawing rooms

the sky imitates with its pinks & blues
a cheap religious painting
the sound system backgrounding with

the Young Cannibals' biggest hit
amplified for The Oasis' forty decks
built into its limestone cliffs

look out & over a shining Lake Travis
where motorboats furrow the waters
while the crowd awaits a bell

will ring down an orange-pink ball
when all will pause from impressive talk
stop sucking on daiquiris or piña coladas

at tables with dips & tortilla chips
to applaud as it sinks below the hills
leaving its unearthly afterglow

know it because on occasion have shown
this sight to out-of-town visitors
who say it is unforgettable

but personally much prefer
to drive after supper
far as the marina at Anderson Mill

to turn around & head unhurriedly back
by Libby's Dance Hall & the mysterious sign
reads among the mesquite "Alma de mujer"

to cross the concrete bridge spans Cedar Creek
as it works its way around deep-bronze rocks
back of a spooky house for private parties

take the curves through a thickly wooded patch
of pecan & sycamore form a roof of leaves
cools in sweltering summer down twenty degrees

then climb to the open twilight
turn west on a road where off to the right
peacocks strut among goats & guineas

on the left a ranch with barbed-wire fence
where by a live oak stand
cattle still graze against the fading light

chewing cuds & staring big-eyed
at a car pulls over & parks
a single longhorn looking up

moving slowly indifferently
knowing he's the one & only
though among the yucca & thistle in bloom

a barely visible doe will appear
first one fawn & then a pair
& then as if out of nowhere

through a thicket of brush & scrub
statue still in silhouette
an antlered buck will peer

the sky lit by a sliver of moon
then back turn & aim the brights
where across the pasture headlights catch

their luminous eyes   suddenly
even more will enter the meadow
while the heavens' herd glimmers above

Bert's Barbecue

once more have waited
far too late
to list the credits due

pay respects to one who
has made it all come back
as only now it dawns

on stepping in between
two sets of picnic benches
ten in all with space enough

for first one leg & then the other
over the seat & underneath
this bare wood pine plank table

with its knifed
names & initials
Amy + JD   Okie   Beto (of

Los Fairlanes could it be?)
Vs vibrating out from a
knot as if in shock

each built by him & his dad
& now for blocks around
the smoke from burning oak

scents this winter air
with chicken beef & ribs
has since 1970

at this alley
intersects with
MLK

after father Johnson
came from Scandinavia
to settle first in New Sweden

then moved the family here to Austin
a master carpenter turned to barbecue
to make a living

gone even longer than Bert
long before such friends as these
Tom Bob Ricardo & Don

have come for his famous food
for lunchtime talk of academics
to join with brokers

bricklayers programmers
secretaries plumbers
students & police

each group in its regular place
with filled cups & paper plates
as overhead Mickey rounds third base

to teammates' pats & handshakes
a homer along with trophies photographed
antlered heads & horns of steers

here too on his in-laws' side
grandfather Adams enshrined
in this city's softball Hall of Fame

while Bert in bib apron
is pictured serving up
cole slaw brisket & beans

catering to *políticos*
like Lyndon Baines
attending too to Lady Bird

whose fruit trees & wildflowers
beautify Interstates & nature trails
she another Johnny Appleseed

but the patrons here more into
pouring on the Cajun sauce
seated beneath

a prospector pans for gold
next to a wide-mouth bass
a giant armadillo of papier-maché

their hats & coats they've hung upon
walls with welded railroad spikes
or hooks of horseshoe nails

framed squaws bending over
their blackened pots
stoking an outdoors fire

watched over by
Geronimo
armed & ready

beside a shot from a John Wayne film
another of a high school football game
where Bert is driving his model-A

from its rumble seat
white-gloved Sweethearts wave
is shown too with Gus-ball lineups

or in his burnt-orange & white suspenders
stands all alone above the rack
for Fritos & Lays potato chips

but features most of all for Texas fans
those moments from Royal's career
when Speyer his speedy receiver

outraced a UCLA defender
outstretched still for hauling in
the winning pass or that epic scene

on Turkey Day against the Aggies
as Worster his wishbone back
plunges off tackle & barrels through

or the legendary season of '69
the Cotton Bowl vs. Notre Dame
with the ball on the Irish 10

4th & 2:26 on the clock & down by 3
the Coach with his headphones on
calling time to confer with Street

his quarterback whose surprising toss
caught 'em off guard & across the room
a facing frame of players leaping

arms signaling the score has brought it home
this tradition still is carried on
by Joyce his wife of thirty-two years

Gary his son an avid sportsman too
who slices the fat
& chats of hunting

of pitches fast or slow

Leukemia & the River of Light

had to go
& pay respects
took some chili con carne & cantaloupes

but dreaded not knowing
what to say
had barely met her folks

though she had come to the house
cheerful even without her hair
fully aware the end was near

had once kept her younger sisters
the time Elisa wasn't able to sit
who always did but on that day

had a track meet out of town
so sat them while her mother stayed
by her hospital bed on into the night

while her stepfather drove to work
then discovered after he'd picked them up
the older had left her dolly behind

on returning it the chubby one answered the door
& on ringing their bell she did again
then welcomed by the mother

the living room filled with greeting friends
some with cold cuts still in their mouths
one breast-feeding as the boxer chewed

his rawhide bone
the kitchen table littered
with flowers & food

took a seat & looked
from face to face
none showing outwardly any sign of grief

then recognized his sculpted head
Dante Alighieri done in whitish stone
his two-foot replica bust

the stepfather saying
it had been his dad's
said it was frightening at night

on arriving late & seeing it stare
so lifelike there at the picture window
as if someone outside were peeking in

seemed not to know the poet's name
thought it cast from concrete
to the touch felt far too smooth

tried speaking of anything else
while he petted his insistent pup
till saying goodbye would come away

relieved on finding that Florentine there
lending even with his dated Paradiso
faith enough to feel

they all were in his care
his medieval eyes lighting the way
to where his Beatrice awaited her

Starting Over
                    for Liz Burkart

your nightmare a mother's dream come true
of a teenage daughter returned once more
to her breast as when a tender babe

though never by a brain stem torn
a collision would send you back to Go
to lie in coma those five long months

each day to await your second birth
to wonder if you'd collect your senses
a joyless pregnancy with little hope

fearing you'd never walk or talk
a pain beyond the hardest labor
as if bearing at once all six of you

off Florida Street just down from where
the city had moved Harry James's home
would run the mile for a merit badge

dashing near your house in that cul-de-sac
later to knock at the door & ask your dad
for a trumpet lesson or parts for brass quintet

finding there each year another face peered up
yours perhaps hidden behind his baggy slacks
could not have picked you out from all the rest

till now you've made us each step back
to recognize & praise any day with legs
have gained again the speed & distance

render thanks for tones the lips can phrase
as your progress slows to the terrible twos
of getting into everything & screaming no

only rolling over with a student's aid
then on your own despite a dark prognosis
still repeating deep within a bright determined yes

or "gabbing away" with a blind board's alphabet
while volunteers fix your hair
as they paint your full-grown infant toes

with your promising art career now on hold
demoted to a one-hand weaving course
yet in John have caught a camping lover

has earned along with you the meaning all over
of sand & gravel of grass & floor
of the touch of every place & hour

sending to all with your one good arm
a signal readies for the taking of marks
getting set not to qualify nor even to win

but merely to record a best time ever

Isabella's Pebbles

barefooted she repeats the word
over & over pebble pebble pebble
wonder why perhaps because

at sixteen months
she thinks by this
to count so many

not even both hands
can hold them all
these shoveled & spread

for a walk between
her *abuelita*'s salvia beds
watered & now inviting

fingers & thumbs to dig
in soft dark mud
can stick to her skin

unlike her fascinating gravel
hard dry & solid
will never wilt

as leaves she picks
or the yellow corollas
she pulls & sniffs

says the word again
with each fist full
then lets them fall

drop one by one
to join their fellows
on the garden path

gathers up some more
then repeats as if
Demosthenes upon the shore

teaching himself to speak
against the Mediterranean roar
though she's been sternly warned

never to put them in
her tiny mouth
then gabbles the word again

one of her first
so far a favorite
& maybe it's since

there seems no end
to shapes & colors
beneath her feet

so smooth to the touch
its sound the same
as all it names

though soon enough will know
if not the geology
has made them be

the way they're called
in her mommy's Spanish
her daddy's Portuguese

besides this Texas English
she insists on saying over & over
who has heard all three

from the lips of parents
were brought together like these
mysteriously from out of the many

when goddess-like she returns
to a special pair
an oblong white

& a tannish pink
her sharp eye spotting
selecting & placing each

in this larger palm
to keep them safe
for a secret need

At the Surplus Supply

a shadow cast
by a lone pecan
makes welcome shade
in this August heat

when a slight
breeze helps to bear
the waiting here
where the used furniture

has found its way
out of date
cracked & chipped
a broken leg

cyclopian computers
blinded as if by an
Odyssean stake
all having landed in

this warehouse of
the institutional discard
though at times
an item will be

recycled & upon a
day like this
one in need
of table or chair

comes to look them over
those have been replaced
to view them once it opens
waiting beneath this single tree

its rough bark coated with
a curry-colored lichen
limestone at its roots
standing here outside

in the midst of slabs
rusting metal in orange &
red gradations beside the
drought-bleached grass

now stunted & stiff
the research labs nearby
for structural engineering
or archeological digs as

it drops Algonquian fruit
for those will hunt & shell
for baking pies & pralines
a taste forever satisfies

whose cool relief from
a blinding summer sun
can never get enough of
will never go out of style

Vincent at the Wal-Mart Supercenter

the woman writing a check
for 45 dollars & 46 cents
the amount visible to all in line
in black against the eerie green
on the register's monitor screen
her hair beginning to thin
along the part in dyed red strands
have lost their sheen
her navy blazer gaping open
down the back where along the seam
its threads are working loose
has in her shopping cart
his Montmartre café scene
with a sticker reads five ninety-nine
the price of this matted print
slashed for faster sale
more than he ever made
from rich shades & luxurious shapes
will enliven her dull apartment wall
his Paris night of flickering stars
above the sidewalk tables & chairs
romance at the extravagant cost
of that ear he razored off
quickly or did he slowly slice
to lessen or increase the pain
& whoever for the skies he daubed
his brush-stroked fields
his trees & swirling birds
would have paid for them
with a pistol to the temple
have squeezed the trigger
for this cityscape
while she has piled it in
along with shampoo
& conditioner in one

snacks soft drinks & panty hose
surely he would've given it away
knowing how much she needs
to escape her advancing age
her worn & fraying outfit
with a bank account
if not overdrawn can barely
afford the cheapest art

Pulling Weeds for Princess Di

Labor Day 1997

this yard work will never end
for these of an unknown nomenclature
will come again

persistent & more profuse
than even the Paparazzi who
hounded you on their motorcycles

when the chauffeur after taking a drink
drove you to that Parisian tunnel
& its unexpected rendezvous

yet surely you knew how all
will even hurt the ones they love
just as these insistent plants

will soon return
to ruin this delicate look
spreads from March or April

as late even as September when
unwanted weeds will still shoot up
through lantana's greening leaves

beside its clean white blossoms
aspiring with unseemly seeded stems
to a royalty & a beauty

they were never meant to achieve
& yet like these the tabloid readers
still need your classic flowering face

the freshness of your mythic name
to approach if only just so near
as a newsprint page

though never so close as
Mother Teresa's curative touch
of the outcast & mutilated

surely you must have known
this irresistible intrusive longing
is the burden of

such loveliness
how those who chased you down
for the photos stained with blood

would grant to you
& each voracious eye
your perennial renewing spring

Tears

have never even half believed
in any the Country & Western sings
the ones jerked by Disney scenes
now those are more my speed

have shed them for tales in technicolor
of Uncle Remus in *Song of the South*
even those with Well shet my mouth
of twin sisters serendipitously discover

a way to trap separated parents belong
together yet prefer metaphors wrung
in Crashaw's rich religious rhymes
his discordant metaphysical hymns

to the Virgin Mother's pitiful dew
descending & gathering at dawn
on the rose petal's blushing hue
dried by a sexed-up caressing sun

not some cowboy weeps in his beer
his tragedy relived at a roadside bar
too late to recover his lucky star
hopefully if she happens to hear

she won't listen to his whining plea
that she give him one last chance
won't let him out of his blue jean pants
when he swears You're the only one for me

even if the record's another gold
its lyrics of leaving her all alone
staggering to find she isn't home
his broken heart it's always sold

more recently couldn't hold them back
such an unpent-up unmanly flow
from viewing *The King of Masks*
rented at the Hollywood Video

& for only a dollar ninety-four
its box with Thumbs Up praise
fined if unreturned on or before
midnight Thursday i.e. five days

watched after having eaten snow pea
tips at the Sea Dragon II a restaurant
run by a Vietnamese once a refugee
in an island camp then immigrant

here where buying a telephone
card can call up that native land
to sobbing kinsmen left behind
in that war-torn romantic zone

having passed over blockbuster hits
PGs can make any actor a millionaire
selected an aging street-performer artist
who searches for a boy to be his heir

for carrying on his line's tradition
its secret of faces replaced so quick
none can see how he puts one on
another off & he will not sell his trick

to soldiers insist he join with Liang
female impersonator of Bodhisalva
who's well off from roles he's sung
a princess moves to cymbaled opera

now the old master enters the market
where the children are sold as slaves
picks a girl who's naturally without
a male's teapot spout & later raves

101

he's been deceived throws her a bag
of coins then pushes off his dinghy
paddles away she wading out to beg
unable to swim then beginning to sink

at last he relents dives in to save her
of course in time she'll do the same
his Doggie will become his rescuer
his faithful female bears that cruel name

but before this takes her to see Liang's
stylized performance in *Beimang Peak*
where the fate of the princess' father hangs
on the appeal of her lachrymal cheek

but the Buddhist patriarchs adhere-
ing strictly to heaven's law condemn
him to the pit of death unwilling to hear
her defense of how a wicked min-

ister laid a trap all rejecting her threat
she'll cut the rope that holds her over
the flames & fall to them from her Boat
of Kindness as later Doggie will hover

above the crowd gathered to plead
for the General to release from jail
her boss her master he who's freed
though only through her sacrificial

act but naturally caught in the nick
of time by Liang in drag yet changes
the officer's mind & the old artist's
too who his "granddaughter" thanks

for turning the trick hugging his dragon
no shrimp would toy with as crystal
drops the pellucid gems began to fall
until from starry eyes the arroyos ran

A Funeral in Brock Texas

the husband of a cousin had died
as a boy had lived next door to her
till moved away at the age of nine
felt obliged to go & pay respects
to attend another unctuous service
on the heavenly host & all the rest

went as much for his sake as hers
he a Native American quiet & kind
both so reticent were only together
through a blind date others arranged
eloped against her mother's wishes
the marriage enduring for fifty years

the church of a two-toned sandstone
erected in '39 the date engraved into
its v-shaped front above the entrance
where a mortuary's man & woman
in black suits smiled good morning
flowers at the altar the casket open

pianist & a handsome music minister
began it with "How Great Thou Art"
his voice surprisingly under control
seminary trained & had come to assist
the Baptist pastor who after the solo
said Let us pray as he bowed his head

afterwards asked for all to rise & join
in singing "Standing on the Promises"
following the hymn a review of the life
employed as a plumber though studied
art in college fought in Korea returned
to work for his dad to build their home

of his own design to become a deacon
a Christian in deed who lived religion
rarely saying a word but when he did
never against but always to encourage
the reverend then to urge his survivors
to carry on His faithful servant's ways

assuring his wife with verses selected
from Nehemiah how she'd have a wall
around her still with support of family
& friends members of their fellowship
should go right on knowing but a husk
remained his soul was with the saints

at the cemetery his metal coffin draped
with stars & stripes graveside ceremony
closing with "Amazing Grace" as slowly
the morticians folded the flag given to her
she receiving it with her habitual silence
a consoling ritual never thought to accept

Entering East Texas From the West

for Margery Pitts Meehan

after Hearne & Marquez
comes Centerville where
the signs begin

sweet gum & pine
wild hog hunting
archery only

the names of towns
Shady Grove & Arbor
at Old Zion a cemetery

at New Hope too
& of course
at Missionary Gospel Church

walkers along the road
dangling from hands
their cans of bait

their long cane poles
riding on shoulders
descendants of those

followed the wagons
the oxen pulled for 28 days
from Mississippi

here to Harmony
& before that Nacogdoches
whose tales she's heard

from relatives moved to
this land of milk & honey
where a wounded infantryman

after discharge in '65
came to be the highest bidder
for a boxed supper

Pernettie Obedience fixed
eaten together
then hitched because

she was in that Rebel's words
as good a cooker
as she was a looker

Strokes

how fathom their coming
from some mysterious where
the when or why of
their sudden stoppage
can numb one side
leave half a self
to stumble its way
the other at times
forever lost in a
black hole swallows
mobility & speech
though memory remains
of what it was
to walk or talk

while watering her yard
parched & wilting from
the rainless weeks
the heat so unrelenting
it made her faint
Aunt Sis fell into flowers
then crawled to the phone
dialed her older daughter
who came in time
but still she complains
she knows the word
but just can't get it out
her sentences slowed
some for sure though
not enough to keep her
from telling again
of the trip they took
to the Pacific coast
of who said what
of the antique bought

in the attic now
could find it if
the pull-down stairs
were not so steep
her knees in such bad
shape at ninety what
can any expect

           yet Gloria
nowhere near her age
called out her student's
name as another teacher
followed instructions on how
to handle violence between
the high school's rival gangs
knew something was wrong
but almost made it through
the rest of the day
then collapsed with feeling
in her left arm gone
now comes & goes
next month will take
early retirement
to travel with Bill
her *schatzie* of thirty-five years
to see Cologne together again
speak the German learned
in her New Braunfels home
its verbs return but then
they're gone

           while Wukasch
holds his useless hand
with a white sock wrapped
around fingers once could
draft architectural plans
for stained glass windows
platt preservation of historic
landmarks a grocery store
a pharmacy a tailor shop
now stares for hours

at the family photo
on his rest home wall
shakes & points with
his one good hand
grunts tee tee tee
at the grandchild there
the blonde with glasses
angered to hear
any other's name
his guardian daughter's
most of all
won't watch TV
for five years now
in a wheelchair with
bowels he can't control
who once harangued
the mayor & city council
to save the decaying sites
who saw his sons & daughters
through college degrees
paid for instruments played
in their string quartet
the four all came last week
to perform "Greensleeves"
in his narrow room
with its institutional meals
for him who knew the Ring
the Rhine's fine wines
the Holy Land seen
with his Anita who visits
whenever she can
though forced by taxes
to divorce her Gene
can her talking & reading
mean a thing to him
does he understand
yet keep it all
locked up inside
with none can find
the key to open
his opulent mind

In Upstate New York a Texas Composer Has Lost His Home

this retreat & sunless escape became
his displaced music's needed landscape
of layered hills & quilted fields
marked off by maples in cold bare rows
angled to darkening clouds in crescendoes
echoed by those lower in distant mist

while nearer this two-storey country house
(called Skåne after that ancestral province
of a grandfather wrote fine English prose
though by every other Swedish immigrant
kidded in Dekker for his heavy accent)
snow holds on out the porch's windows

facing east & west & south
to his winding downhill stone-
bordered shale-covered drive
& below to a pond's ice-blinded
opaque pupil whose melted edges
mirror skeletal limbs & mobile sky

as leaf-littered banks contrast
with patches of muddied ground
or of greening mounds of grass
a pair of lifting & falling willows
their thin branches a yellow writhing
against a stand of wet black trunks

squirrels racing out along their boughs
birds dipping or gliding in circles tighten
pheasant & deer now out of sight
have strutted brightly or bounded through
an unmown plot of frozen asters
plants nibbled till the garden fenced

110

took bankruptcy to keep this adopted scene
to set down its blustery overcast sound
would take as if by winter storm
the city's unavoidable concert halls
counter the noise & grime & ridicule
to earn too a return for arias in June

but in the end foreclosure has come
to evict the artist from his quiescent view
perhaps for the best in forcing him back
on memories of Dekker or a New Gulf youth
where despite inevitable loss with every gain
inspiration began & still can & will sustain

On Rehearing Aaron Copland's Orchestral Variations During the 100th Anniversary of the Composer's Birth

for Karl Miller

when music inspired something said
to pattern words the same
though noun interpose where its
verb or intended meaning sounds
sense wrong for the song

inspired when music said something
to sense words for sounds
where the same noun or
verb though its meaning wrong
song interpose the intended pattern

music said something inspired when
sounds though intended for sense
pattern words verb or noun
to where the wrong meaning
interpose its song the same

when something inspired music said
pattern song to its sense
though wrong where the same
words noun or verb interpose
the sounds intended for meaning

said something inspired when music
though words wrong to meaning
interpose the same noun or
verb where song pattern its
sounds for the intended sense

something said when music inspired
pattern the same sounds verb
or noun to where though
wrong for the meaning words
intended sense interpose its song

Of "Guernica" for Solo Viola by William Penn

a contemporary composers show on PBS
the announcer asks the obvious
Descended from that Quaker man?
Answer: No relation
took his doctorate at 31
went to Western Michigan

the same conference as N.I.U.
played them football in drifting snow
cold schooling in Kalamazoo
so numbing with temperatures sub-zero
Spain is south & in the sun
Answer: No relation

the soloist a sophomore
a mere 3 weeks he had the score
Performance: near flawless
Penn explains: women weep bombs fall the whole mess
afterwards ears perk up at every note
wonder most at how warm he wrote

Civil War for viola the instrument right
a mellow wooden box subtler as it soars
melody out of massacre
with runs reach for the light
marvel at the mind the musician admire
a queer relation William Penn & war

how could an American know the score
how connect the long pass with Picasso
how did Guernica take it stopping for college at 10 below
Kalamazoo
& viola too
a wet-behind-the-ears sophomore

has cartoon America learned to feel
sounds unreal
yet heard it even as wind the flakes did blow
what's more on radio
with Larry Dutton violist & special thanks to Wm.'s pen
a music-making has made Kalamazoo & Pablo   kin

Three Musicians Perform Their Freedom

each so distinct
in dress & instrument
a trio so intent
in spite of the fact
the paraphernalia in
this bookstore-espresso café

must needs distract
from the vital statement
they have come to make
since the clothes each wears
or goes without these too
take away from the effort

for ears to hear how free
their expression is
or dreams to be
the bassist leader in his
mod glasses shirt & tie
with close-cropped hair

bows first then plucks
his fingers acrobatic upon
the four tuned strings
quoting the Mingus theme
from "Isabel's Table Dance"
on that '57 *Tijuana Moods*

while the percussionist's one
bare foot presses the pedal
his short-sleeved shirt of
collarless African design with
diamond lines russet & black
coordinating with faded jeans

kicks with his kit of
two snares bass & tom tom
his thin golden cymbals
ringing delicately from
sticks hit lightly against
their oval rims

the vocalist's lips
releasing her tones in sync
with cymbals & strings
sounds from deep within
up through her throat & out
between her brightened teeth

eyes closed as she fidgets
with a right-hand ring
her concentrated attempt
in spite of all she knows
must call attention to looks
instead of wordless notes

her black tight-fitting attire
a cocktail style with spaghetti
straps cleavage & angled skirt
lower in front than back
though none of this intended
to upstage the urgent song

yet even her face with no
make-up her high-heeled
sandals & painted nails
her turquoise necklace
the sinfully delicious
sign for gourmet rolls

behind & to her side the
whir of a mocha machine
these too now interfere
with the trio's heroic
endeavor to deliver
the message of

music's liberation to
consumer conscious
& fashion aware

The Pilgrimage

began at 7:20 a.m. Austin-Bergstrom
December 20th two thousand & one
on American flight number 24 0 9
two planes that airline lost
on September 11th to terrorism
brought the Twin Towers down
though in a way it began in '59
when *Pulse* printed that essay on him
as a pioneer & later wrote in '61
"Order of Worship" that early poem

at first María felt too afraid to fly
then feared it would be too far to drive
weather in the east so unpredictable
the car without any chains or snow tires
tickets bought in August nonrefundable
but in the end decided she would risk it
even willing at last to leave alone
on December 10th for Avon
to help Elisa with Christmas
the granddaughters turning 3 & 6

ten days later would join them all
Newton & Darío & Jennifer too
landed in Hartford where at Nook Farm
Twain had written *The Gilded Age*
Stevens walked to work up Asylum Hill
but never managed to see either one
with only a week & most of the days
filled with observing the girls at play
fighting over who would carry the cat
yet determined at least to take that trip

Jenny would baby-sit the younger sister
Newton said he'd seen the town before
on traveling I-84 to meet with clients
in his job with National Instruments
the rest would pack into Elisa's van
head down the roadway lined with pine
here & there a birch with whitest bark
past the campus of a community college
named Tunxis after an Indian tribe
could imagine its wild idyllic life

among the woods on either side
outcroppings of a reddish rock
Darío saying he'd heard or read
how for such a very rich state it had
the highest percentage of working poor
remembered then the tourist brochure
on Connecticut's "Quiet Spaces"
the composer's disappointment in '39
on visiting his once "lively" birthplace
found it so changed had never returned

yet still came hoping to view his home
the Housatonic Valley inspired his "grand
and glorious noise" just then passing over
its river known from his aural depiction
in his vivid *Three Places in New England*
brought back a synesthetic vision of bands
marching & playing their differing strains
crossing & creating a polytonal dissonance
captured in notes he had set down at night
as with Stevens after a day of insurance

stopped for directions at a service station
a Pakistani saying keep on White to Main
turned left & parked at the Savings Bank
where bells of the Congregational Church
once rang out of tune such a delight to him
& his father who on piano had copied them
both hearing the gospel across Chapel Place

at now Danbury National Bank at 210 Main
born on the spot in '74 & living there till '79
when the family moved to the intersection of

Stevens Street with Harmony there till '89
then back to Chapel Place's renovated barn
listening for five years before leaving for Yale
just a paved parking lot the only thing there
the homestead pump organ & steeple gone
the house moved to South & Mountainville
got back in the van & continued up Main
after missing the sign with his faded name
turned around & found his desolate home
the 1790 Dutch colonial in need of paint

pulled into the drive behind a panel truck
from it a workman emerged would prove
unfriendly when asked for a peek inside
said "There's nothing here" yet advertised
the carved music stand a gift of his wife
his death mask & on-loan Pulitzer Prize
took one photograph in that dimming light
then Darío insisted we locate the grave
so drove at dusk in search of a Section M
in the cemetery where beside his Harmony

Charles now lies overlooking the pond
yet couldn't find it gave up & went on
to Dunkin' Donuts to use its restroom
where a teenager with a ring in her nose
brought back how prophetic that street
with her very same name though to most
instead of Harmony had married discord
at best only repeating snatches of hymns
quoting again "The Battle Cry of Freedom"
or "Come Thou Fount of Every Blessing"

with Elisa at the wheel peered out in the dark
at Waterbury's lights on passing back through
wondering if by any chance the Pakistani knew

his *Concord Sonata* if that teenager were to hear
his symphonies or *Robert Browning Overture*
would she convert to faith in the transcendental
from body piercing since not even to have seen
stand or gravestone reverence had been renewed
& in Texas would soon put on *The Unanswered
Question* & "In the Barn" from his *Sonata #2*

Extra Virgin

with eight straight
record-setting days
of over a hundred degrees

contemplate in the comfort
of Styx river
air conditioning

this square plastic
Bertolli bottle with
its two indented sides

for holding on to by
fitting into them
fingertips & thumb

spreading the palm
across its label
bears the name of

that Tuscan town
Dante condemned
to his Circle Eight

Lucca's grafters dipped
in boiling pitch
like bits of meat

its letters framed by
two girls facing each
innocent & ageless

with hair cut short
their skirts hiked up
to bended knees

their bare arches
curved against the
trunks of trees

having shinnied up
now hang by hands
one from a limb

the other reaching
among the leaves
have since 1865

the same year
that Civil War
came to an end

though still not the
de facto manumission
date too of the first

cold pressing of its
rich black fruit for
a salad dressing

for luscious chiabatta
loaves baked with it locally
for serving with Siena

or Hill Country wine
this liter of oil filtered
to a clarity little refined

for retaining the
flavor recalls his
Commedia divine

his Inferno's pure
delicious wickedness
imported here

deep in the heart
of this hellish
Texas heat

Mountains

can lift the spirits whenever they're low
while some just scale their haughty heights
to show them or their alpinist rivals below
Dante climbed Purgatory to purge his soul
poets used to appeal to a Parnassian muse
though in place of myths of Jupiter & Zeus
they now mean ski lifts & Olympic gold
in New Mexico many have looked up to
the Sangre de Cristo as a sacred range
where the Rockies' snow has yet to melt
an earthly promise of the eternal self
sun however on an ermine cold can change
the ice to river rage requires a dam's control
yet its energy charge not one the Incans felt
camping on slopes of smoking Andean peaks
only pacified by their leaving a virgin to freeze
Tiwa carved petroglyphs of kokopelli's flute
down from Sinai Moses brought a Decalogue
tablets engraved for being read & lived up to
from a distance seem to rise but never move
unmoved even by the great or a simple faith
by all the prayers are offered night & day
answering only with another lava flow
quakes shaking & taking the towns away
whole cultures buried in preservative dust
suffocating those who wrote graffiti on love
ruins still breathing a long-dead Vesuvian art
from sight of Popocatepetl some never depart
in spite of fears staying on for seasonal views
the elevating histories & purple majesty hues
Texans renewed by driving hundreds of miles
to the Guadalupe remote from computer files

A Texas Version of Crèvecoeur

in the *Letters* of that eighteenth-
century farmer men like plants
ingest their nature as inhabitants
of the air they happen to breathe

yet flourish best by taking root
in soil untilled for earl or baron
any land they can call their own
transplanted here from Europe

the Czechs still brought along
the names of towns back home
painted Praha's church the same
echoing too with Catholic song

but with their communities gone
to cities since any youth escapes
their steeples now all rise alone
settlers at rest in nearby graves

forgotten until the camera crew
revisit such sites for Public TV
to capture an intricate imagery
in sanctuaries the faithful knew

the pink granite Capitol built
by stonemasons highly skilled
in a trade they had carried over
from auld & bonny Edinburgh

freed slaves erecting mansions
after southern style plantations
laying track through eastern pine
swinging blues boogie & ragtime

famed more for rattlers & rednecks
chili cook-offs the cattle & crude
yet one can find any foreign food
such distinctive dresses & dialects

in Nederland now the Cajun live
Germans serve braten in Gruene
Mexican shops offer the votive
most towns feature Thai cuisine

in houses down at Bolivar beach
find Mazzus Parigis & Costanzas
like Neapolitans so loved to fish
whose airs inspired opera's arias

but unlike the returning buffalo
no more roaming Karankaways
those replaced by a mix of races
of Arabs & Brazilians come & go

Chinese Japanese & Taiwanese
heard on the street or in recital
Buddhist weddings Bach gigues
all harvesting in a heat unpastoral

mingled & separate the new & old
once poet Constantin Kuzminsky
or a critic like Sudhakar Jamkhandi
enriching more than any black gold

while in this garden in Cedar Park
a Chilean tends her mountain laurel
with its native blossom leaf & bark
reciting laureates Neruda & Mistral

All Thumbs

Bronowski in his writings on
man's ascent has said he expends
more gray matter manipulating
these than even on
the chest & abdomen

with a cut on the right
it was painful to hit
the notes in any line of
Bach's two-part invention
number six

when J.S. came on the scene
it was they say
the least used digit
wonder how without it
they could even play

once it healed still
could not bring off his trills
& ornaments at half
a Glenn Gould's
slowest speed

it is one thing makes
the species unique
animal-like & yet can be
not cruel only
but full of justice

down for death up for life
opposed to the index
precisely   sucked   green
stuck out to hitch a ride
bent to push this pen

Poets Teachers & a Librarian

Fessing Up to David Yates

> Ure aeghwylc sceal   ende gebidan
> worolde lifes   *—Beowulf*

miss you most because   & must admit it
your magazine meant   a place to publish
a form of self-love   a by-line craved as ever
though more so now   than ever before
since at your going   your tabloid folded
had opened to   the priceless poems
at times a photo   when you chose to run it
of your own face's inner glow   no mirror can ever return
that final number's pose   white hair long & premature
though no sign there   of a ruptured disc
the pain or pills   could push you instead of proofing
through the press   to pump the exhaust fumes in

would await the mail   for each new issue
to find unknowns   their metaphors oh so fresh
could make the day   or save it from
a feeling any food   fast or grown organic
is such a waste   can never really feed
as words you penned   of a recipe for making bread
of a cow skull's smile   from brushing its yellowed teeth
on Dickey's independence   his speech to all
then flopped facedown in   the middle of the street
when he's put to bed by friends   to sleep it off
or the elderly ignored   Stafford's story of snickersnee
West Texas Wind   which you compared to sex
need them more & more   yet must confess
poets as good have appeared   even then were here
but your editing & imprint   there's none to replace
a where to write   to your Madeline address
its road overlooking   your logo's rock & cedar
receiver of manuscripts   of hopeless lines

held close in hands to drink them in   when all the others
shot them back   you alone would send acceptance

ask shamefully then   that you forgive & forget
though cannot do   the same for you
unable to live   with the way you left
who in public had written   to stay in touch
but even failed to phone   to listen to Leon's
take a later flight   pulling out so sudden-like
the red flag not yet up   ticks still on the meter
as any Minute Man   each would've dropped & run
assembled as the Amish   at a clanging bell
now grieve image-loss   on a newsprint page
the inked-up verses   a vital life-blood
an obsession yes   the one you set aside
yet a rejection slip   can still not read

Murphey's Law

whatever could & did go wrong
would by-&-by turn into song
that was it the long

& short of Joseph Colin's law
part Indian but which tribe Choctaw
or Cherokee didn't rightly know

wore turquoise around his wrist over a skin
glowed at the cheekbones younger year in
year out   the seasoned subtle poetry written

never showing its slow-talking maker's age
no bitterness self-pity nor rage
over a father's common-law ménage

or his poet's mind ignored
by that Irishman he dreamed still undivorced
though knew & accepted had left his mother had even whored

Joe tenured yet after the academic dean had plagued
him daily teaching in Huntsville at Sam Houston State
resigned for shift work at a packing plant then selling real
                                        estate

but even in Dumas the ding-dong-daddy rhymes & rhythms
                                        came
as with "Panhandle Piety" he'd sit at the table forever the same
blessing whatever was served in that neglectful father's name

in Gainesville celebrating an earlier owner's suicide
restringing his wire had endured long after he died
believing his bad buried & his good alive in that home he made

135

discovering through a skunk raided their henhouse there
the artist as perfect hero taking from him the full measure
of his death-defying pride in the face of unattainable treasure

his rich odor worth more than those Seven Cities of Gold
a writing survives on the strength of Texas lives his lines retold
stories so strong can't lose the trail   won't ever grow cold

To James White Bear Cody

it wasn't the death
you must have dreamed
of being left behind
by the Tonkawa tribe
under live oak pine
or some other tree
to sit beneath it
& await the descent
of that Great Spirit
would lift you up
to happy hunting grounds

instead your truck turning
at the signal light
with the setting sun
right in your eyes
foot surgery slowing reaction
braking late leaving behind
loves of your life
the Korean artist wife
a daughter of five
an unfinished doctoral thesis
poems still to revise

Thanks to Behlen for the Anderson

mailing Michael's chapbook
a copy of *The Road, The Eye*
Charlie Bill you sure came through
with your promised gift
to replace this title missed

had lent it to another friend
but was never returned by him
you much more thoughtful then
true to your word in giving needed
Texas poems you said you'd send

To Marshall Rick Roderick

with your West Texas accent
as thick as it comes
& your prickly cacti witticisms
it shocked one to learn how you went
as far & as high as you did
amazed how Duke could endure
you for those seven long years
till a committee of your so-called peers
convened deliberated & duly denied
you university tenure

but then you'd lost before & would again
as when on Tuscola's baseball team
you got your high school butt beat off
by tiny Baird or biggie Abilene
your girlfriend with her life cut short
did that make you a philosopher king
a master teacher of Platonic thinking
of German Wilhelm & Danish Søren
those with a will or a faith to leap
were you dreaming them in your final sleep

it takes a loser like you & your Socrates
to serve as a gadfly or a pigskin critic
to question a defense every coach believes
will win & to accept no answer is academic
or pedantic & as for pay well forget it
unless one wants to be exploited
by extension courses or community college
classes barely funded by a pork barrel Lege
you knew all this from Hume & Mill
was it really overwork could suddenly kill

or living in the clouds of your cigarette smoke
a heart taxed by scores from Longhorn games
reading till late *Civilization & Its Discontents*
to raise four sons alone might make one croak
but to you was richer than a forty-niner's claims
& surely you wouldn't have blamed it on books
on critiques of man or any defeat in a sudden-death
overtime after they'd tied it up or on political crooks
maybe altogether yet these in the end were merely hints
at what made you tick your logic took away one's breath

In Memoriam: Winfred S. Emmons

was a practicing Southern Baptist
with an unlikely sense of humor
who loved Geoff Chaucer best
the raunchier he was the better

as when that angry Host bristles
tells the Pardoner he just wishes
he had aholt of his little testicles
says to this peddler of religious

relics charges for kissing a stain
on dirtied drawers he would fain
cut the scrawny pair & enshrine
them both in the turd of a swine

frost on a mule's the metaphor
Win used for that first mustache
tried to grow as his sophomore
next day shaved it by breakfast

selected for his course in British
Lit a Blake-to-present anthology
didn't include "To Nobodaddy"
so he'd recite it all with relish

not too long after he had gone
took down his monograph on
Katherine Anne Porter whose
Texas stories he could choose

over "The Chimney Sweepers"
said the 'weep made it weaker
how disagree with this mentor
who inspired in that '60 winter

to imitate the Yeats he assigned
in the annual from '61 a picture
shows him already with hairline
receding into his perennial burr

one of his Ethel's photographs
he in the front at that decadent
lounging Roman-style banquet
of her high school Latin class

in another at the football game
she's leading a yell in her dead
language Robert Nossen recom-
mended Study with her he said

& did but only a private lesson
or two then left for UT Austin
where had it first from Jim Hitt
then later from Christian Smith

had not learned much from her
too short a time just remember
how she'd apply above the line
of her upper lip a ruby Revlon

as for him can see the twinkle
& hear his high-pitched laugh
on translating the Miller's Tale
when a coed got the paragraph

where Nicolas breaks wind how
Absolon pokes the hot plough-
share & burns off his ers's skin
Nick's love for Alison yqueynt

a jolly prof who knew his stuff
from *Hamlet* to the Dick Tracy
comic strip mostly B.O. Plenty
James Joyce & Virginia Woolf

in his Advanced Grammar gave
a poem to diagram can imagine
the prepositions in sonnet 129
phrasals laid to make one rave

a couplet on his midterm exam
so tricky a claque of classmates
up nights before trying to cram
was one of his special delights

to some such woe proved bliss
others called it a perfect waste
all they wanted was just to pass
saw him as in the way of haste

said wouldn't need it for a thing
didn't plan to teach where else
put it to a single use only hell's
for passives in living & writing

though can't believe he's there
surely he wasn't condemned for
being a wit or inclined to savor
scatalogical rhymes his Despair

unlike Red Crosse knight's saved
by his Una's cutting words from
in *The Faerie Queene* of Book One
giving in to Duessa's rusty blade

Win's from slaving away on half
the pay of a CEO holds no Ph.D.
rendering eke & wight year after
year grading papers so unworthy

losing patience with her atrocious
Thesis then plied a mean red pen
marking it up almost murderous
found him at home with swollen

legs left him sitting sore & bitter
more from being asked to resign
eyes missing their wonted shine
his final days no joking matter

his face minus its devilish grin
had opened & shown so lustily
to interpret a Robert Browning
his Brother he-he snaps the lily

Ethel silent in her nearby chair
their classrooms three blocks
away the blackboards where
both had shared their classics

his "Michael" her Virgil was
this to what it all came down
a form of puritanical justice
for having slighted a religion

by teaching an unholy empire
a gat-toothed lecherous Wife
of Bath then why even aspire
as Nannie says to any afterlife

though this too's just a fiction
of Porter's he had closely read
a black woman's contradiction
of all the church has ever said

whether a parting hour reveal
the comedy's errors are those
told in some Canterbury Tale
or come of believing He arose

what good would it do to say
this merely means to witness
his explications abide & bless
pay homage to his jocular way

Teachers at South Park High

1

those still living invited to that 45th reunion
but of the five attended didn't take from any
one couldn't make it with his aluminum brain

most unheard of since graduation of the many
had departed the favorite having gone the year
before & yet every face has come back funny

or earnest from nine endless months of appear-
ing at the heads of rows for the calling of roll
going over a grammar point & making it clear

all the lessons can't recall to save one's soul
though each body retains what he or she wore
all the quirks & tics days they'd lose control

when interrupted & talked out of turn or more
often the questions unheard too witty to learn
certainly from losers considered a deadly bore

now remembered then merely intent on spurn-
ing not alone subjects but their old fogey look
fashion & make-up meaning most to undiscern-

ing hotshot know-it-alls wouldn't crack a book
to be so cool education wasted would later say
on the young unprepared for reading of a Huck

Finn would start over do it again ready to pay
attention memorize driest dates work equations
yet can only half-regret on a laser-printed page

2

with the aid of crutches & metallic braces
she would walk the halls but once in class
held sway in a wheelchair beside her desk

issuing the instructions in her husky voice
or declaiming the cobbler's comedic lines
surgeon to old shoes mender of bad soles

though her belief in a *Key to the Scriptures*
kept her from consulting a physician when
poliomyelitis had attacked her spinal cord

a wart on her nose recalls the Graymalkin
scene in *Macbeth* Act I though was never
a witch even if her long gray scraggly hair

made her with that growth to look the part
dramatic she was & big on deportment too
had one rule for males to stand up as soon

as any female entered the room to remain
standing until the girl or lady should say
please be seated her laughter deep enough

it could have been heard in Falstaff's inn
made an assignment for giving directions
for reaching one's home some anecdote of

a family sort felt then she was flat wrong
to disapprove that telling of the phone call
from a man asked to speak with Mr. Olfart

3

with her classes she would always share
the memories from those days in Mexico
when the dashing caballero serenaded her

singing from a street below & sending up
fresh roses filled a bathtub in her pensión
would speak too of & even demonstrated

the Mexican hat dance that *jarabe tapatío*
whirled about as her handkerchief twirled
to sounds of the guitar she once had heard

with the old maid's back turned poked fun
at her romantic delusions so unconcerned
with conjugating of any subjunctive verb

pronouncing volcanoes' nostalgic names
making the male & female endings agree
placing of an accent on the proper vowel

what wouldn't give to chat with her now
in that tongue have come to love so well
even blending a gringo's with Latin blood

admit she was right to remember that tub
to wear their colorful embroidered skirts
to have club members peddle Xmas cards

for a trip in winter across the Rio border
didn't go after all but had sold the most
demanding the money from generous her

4

indignant to find any man would teach
a class studs said was meant for sissies
those would elect not to take his course

later to pay for a messy expensive typist
but jeered back then at his potbelly waist
snickered whenever once again he'd stick

his hand in the candy machine while those
who signed up & tried to erase the mistake
were always caught soon as he would hold

yellow sheets to the light & spot the place
where paper was thinner & if any thought
to cut off misspellings he would dig them

out of the trash & for such offenses made
to stand in the hall their heads in lockers
one foot in a wastebasket till hour's end

with gum on noses for those who chewed
carriage returns timed to a record played
his "Blueberry Hill" or "One Mint Julep"

he himself cradling & bowing an air violin
tonguing his finger & touching his cheek
to imitate teardrops of girls would plead

that he not count off for just one erasure
reduced their speed the racier sort invited
to wear baby dolls at his slumber parties

seeing classes listed in a printed schedule
for that spring semester dad read it as if
Plain Gloom were being taught by Bible

though it wasn't he sure got the blues riff
part absolutely right with mimeoed notes
on a depressing hypotenuse predated stiff

twin compasses of a metaphysical poet's
simile for the circle of an unaltering love
hating then every angle this tennis coach

drew obtuse or acute attempting to prove
theorems of equal to less or greater than
bitter most from how he would only have

any patience with cute girls raised a hand
to ask some stupid question later learned
was dismissed for dating coeds even chang-

ing grades from those a cheerleader earned
good looking he was with a dimpled cheek
his players winning under him most tourn-

aments they'd enter but couldn't compete
with his boys on any clay or asphalt court
yet just by giving of extra points he'd beat

them out of the pretty ones none too smart
in the parallelogram triangle or a trapezoid
but knew the horizontal line a passing mark

6

no religious sect the subject of her lectures
even though were studying the King James
version of those old & new holy scriptures

now little more than a Job or Ruth remains
a vague proverb of flattery & fury's snares
spread for neighbors' feet the child shames

dear mother when the unwise father spares
a rod mostly read chronicles of who begets
generations while a wife or concubine bears

for sure the beatitude or parable none forgets
mountain sermon to innumerable multitudes
criticism of the whispering hidden in closets

when the covered's revealed murder & truth
will out as the Nun's Priest's mock rooster
knew so well who listened to a hen & rued it

by then had learned how that later literature
could teach the very lessons & never preach
came to prefer Geoffrey's Canterbury humor

to Paul's epistles filled with their pious peace
which passeth understanding a charity whores
that meek lamby love that constant I beseech

ye sinners to follow me flee o ye fornicators
& did that mild lady ever in virtuous dreams
envision this outcome from her sacred course

with names a quixotic mix of the epic & hick
high-collared blouse & protruding front teeth
a flowery skirt it all made her a laughing stock

as she'd trace Americans by periods & dates
from puritan predestiny through colonial rule
to killing fields of the war between the states

in the summer she would tour the battle sites
Vicksburg's row on row of moss-hung graves
Gettysburg's gentle hills where Confederates

met their match & Abe's two-minute address
said it forever whereas for hours would raise
her voice when none would listen her classes

paying for subscriptions to *Senior Scholastic*
at 10 cents each its quizzes on current events
Nasser seizes Suez Canal the polls favor Ike

vocabulary words drawn from a Soviet block
maps import graphs sports tips on etiquette
letters to the editor the rating of a latest flick

reports on rock & roll rhythms causing riots
on a Nobel Prize discovery in a human heart
thought hers too ancient for having the hots

for any but those had eons ago already died
amazed to learn how late in life she married
had quit teaching to become a blushing bride

his reddish-brown eyes would almost pop out
the whites probably bloodshot from the strain
of glaring when clarinets missed their entrance

did he ever learn those tubas changed the name
of Elsa's *Procession to the Cathedral* dubbing it
her *Outhouse* mostly it was the one who threw

newspapers before & after classes took revenge
on a couple turned him in for tossing them into
their flower beds by taking a dump in a grocery

sack setting it afire leaving it up on their porch
so they'd stomp it out he & his buddies' tricks
the newest boy's sousaphone filled with water

so surprised when he blew & nothing came out
yet polishing bells with pride before each game
when they'd oompah Sousa's *Washington Post*

faithfully rehearsing Rossini's *Italian in Algiers*
a movement of Dvorak's *From the New World*
arranged for concert-band to compete that year

all eyes on him when he'd step to the podium
raising his baton for the intricate opening strain
practiced until mistakes had made him threaten

not to go to contest till the drum major gave his
pep talk with this director out of the room said
all must do their best did & won a lyred-patch 1

9

her hands small with tiny fingers hanging at ends
of short plump nearly doll-sized arms her wrists
with a deep crease from which she would push

continually her pink or light blue sweater sleeves
her narrow shoulders flaked with dandruff snow
her eyes never looking at one but up & fluttering

as seated at her desk in high-heeled slings would
not stay up any more than hand-knitted sleeves
she critiqued any leaning on the lectern allowed

no ums or ahs grading a delivery & presentation
by Monroe's five-step sequence of the attention
getter then need satisfaction visualization action

while her favorites on the forensic team sneaked
her keys said were preparing rebuttals backstage
then crawled through the dressing room window

while class continued drove her car from school
to the downtown beer joints to shoot some pool
parked returned the keys to her purse as the bell

sounded for the period's end did she ever know
maybe all along let them get away with murder
more concerned with enunciation debating either

side researching issues to affirm & negate argue
& win the case such trophies won & displayed
can those make up for showing so little respect

10

on looking back it doesn't seem to mean a thing
yet its parenthetical numerals letters in brackets
two minuses make a plus equal a kind of swing

when at the end the answer to a problem checks
whether one likes reuniting broken bits depends
mostly on who conducts the class if all business

the way she was it can make a fateful difference
especially when no humor is added to the math
not being assigned the best & brightest students

as her colleague was made her resentful perhaps
honor society membership ended by that lower
grade from absence on debate & orchestra trips

of which she disapproved was among her sorer
points so took some off turned B to negative C
but for figuring it out requires a mind far more

adept than one can only solve for X dividing 3
by 5 or 6 placing a decimal on the proper side
multiplying numerators their equation the key

to explain the wholes of fractional parts decide
if by subtracting it would give a greater amount
common complex compound still so mystified

by its being the basis of sound & can account
for every living thing except of course for her
who computed a number that really did count

11

next to last of the dozen years short or long
depending on the point of view the teachers
taken he the first in a field looked to belong

exclusively to the second sex with features
& voices made literature too girlish for boys
his first year & time for ushering preachers

in from Boston's puritanical line the ahoys
of voyages after the godlike whale or back
to a Cotton Mather who compared to sauce

Homer's epic heroes an *Iliad*'s Achilles lack-
ing in Christian virtues true food for thought
but can't recall reading the powers of black-

ness nor was a "Song of Myself" ever taught
not until college scanning subversive *Leaves*
as he of a hillbilly appellation would exploit

his classes having them prepare for speeches
up on stage sawing & hammering set designs
for *Arsenic & Old Lace* or his *Angel Street*'s

student production while Miss Dickinson's
enigmas didn't amaze Walt's barbaric yawp
remained unsounded as Dimmesdale's sins

yet in between painting of scenery & prop
assigned "Old Ironsides" "Concord Hymn"
those first poems made the heart half stop

155

12

was famous for his mercurial Irish moods
slamming down in disgust a stubby baton
on the stenciled music stand when woods

or strings missed his cue not coming in on
time but then on retuning a violin he'd tell
an anecdote a joke on himself the passion

subdued yet to rise again all knew so well
followed by the deep regret endeared him
at least to those placed him on a pedestal

for sounds he brought to life a Beethoven
1st Gershwin's Parisian horns Diz & Bird
for buying Rugolo's *Adventures in Rhythm*

with school system funds swing unheard
until he left his St. Louis home with bop
in tow scatting notes spreading the word

of syncopation rehearsing for a sock hop
Saturday nite though stock arrangements
like "Jersey Bounce" a far cry from pop-

tune rock by a swiveling pelvis students
adored even with dance a sin in the Bible
belt his drinking only a superintendent's

enlightened view defended against a libel
would've had him fired who improvised
on sax blew the mind to jazz & classical

had it been an elective unrequired to graduate
whoever would've chosen to take from him
his course with a title warned will regurgitate

from dissected frogs dots on monarch wings
protect against blue jays learn they're bitter
but even with a microscope lens for looking

at amoeba couldn't see a thing just wonder-
ed if with those thickest glasses he ever saw
the miniscule labels for stirrup anvil hammer

of the ear whose cochleal tubing had to draw
apathetic to which canal led where had rather
hear & play beguine notes of an Artie Shaw

than to know near or farsighted didn't matter
not at all only wanted eye-hand coordination
to read & perform the parts for second chair

can't remember if he taught equine evolution
from three-toed into a single hoof or thought
Darwin mistaken & held to a special creation

by then science knew the DNA if he brought
it up tested spelling enzyme or chromosome
don't recall just phoning of neighbors' daugh-

ters for Saturday dates later the senior prom
struggled to adapt make the natural selection
be different with all cells of the same system

14

her honors classes reserved for talented types
not being one missed out on the inspiring fun
of her course in the fabrication of poetic lives

tracing the piney woods prosaic existence one
was living then & like the others giving the lie
to every prayer & profession of a regular Sun-

day attendance could only glimpse her manly
walk her legs wide apart & somewhat bowed
her glasses hanging below her bosom held by

a chain or ribbon her hairdo not at all in vogue
her voice a little gruff but never heard it speak
of how to shape a story in an off-rhyme mode

recount a tale of boomtown life in a Sour Lake
Saratoga or her native Batson where she lived
& commuted from its scum once called a freak

of nature when it bubbled flared cured arthritis
drew a lawless crew of roustabouts & wildcat
speculators read her '43 thesis on aeronautics

in secondary schools to train the air-age pilot
against the Nazi threat by means of Daedalus
Icarus & Pegasus' dreams of da Vincian flight

learning if late a vocabulary of radio compass
de-icing diving physiological effects of flying
from it & her camping essay literary calculus

like the Wife of Bath in Chaucer's prologue
whose opening verse paragraph memorized
with its rhyming couplets & London brogue

she too was gat-toothed who said it signified
lecherousness but couldn't conceive it in her
so tall overbearing & never even tried to hide

a wart visible in the v of suede or calf leather
pump watched it as she'd read another sonnet
or a Grecian ode more fascinating than either

as she'd drone on followed her foot saw it fit
right in that v better than poets can fill a form
the best assignment she ever gave was Write

an essay on any theme & so this schoolmarm
got a dissertation on snuff after Lamb's roast
pig which unlike a man is good in every part

but of course she found sniffing tobacco most
unacceptable as a subject for an English class
& deducted points for clearly having grossed

her out then book reports due if hoped to pass
when asked if half a 1000-page novel'ld count
since time was running out replied in her sass-

y way you will flunk out of college & amount
to nothing & the shoe did fit but luckily saved
by majoring in lit of many a blessing the fount

what a trip to return to the time of resentment
acne puppy love petty fears lessons forgotten
so many never learned when most were meant

to prepare & lead or steer one to or away from
naïveté not being aware of all there was to live
for without or with the much was yet to come

to keep the mind & options open never to give
up on others or on one's self or less than one's
best effort in every test trial tribulation even if

no grade's assigned or no award is granted once
the task is done the paper completed the course
finished when nothing is ever over only a dunce

would think a past will not catch up & reinforce
the laws & rebukes one thought to have left back
there with those believed too dull & slow hoarse

from repeating that same insistent stupid didac-
tic stuff about not plagiarizing taking good notes
staying up with the reading never being a slack-

er all their sagest counsel ignored in sowing oats
but oh what fun to sneer & feel superior to each
& every one or at least those seeming to be most

out of tune with a hit parade could always teach
more than all their textbooks adopted by a dumb
committee no member of which dared eat a peach

Ex Libris Decherd Turner

started out from Pike County near
Twain's Mississippi but even prior
to his black-Irish birth his mother's
clairvoyant said she could only see

a room full of books & with his last
exhibition the collecting had spread
far from titles he propped on a plow
his Missouri mule pulling as he read

the town's Carnegie would not allow
any country boys to check them out
could only be seen under Ms. Irwin's
watchful eye who one day revealed

a kinsman of hers was a librarian too
yet before he chose that sacred path
married the sweetheart of his youth
ordained a minister by the Seminary

just shelving books to earn a living
then discovering in such holy relics
a gospel he felt was meant to preach
the priesthood of printing on vellum

by the end his labeled exhibit cases
displaying cones with hieroglyphics
once buried under Ashur's temples
typefaces on rag paper straw & silk

a photograph of his own large hands
with inked palms & fingers lettered
as a cheat-sheet aid to remembering
his final speech delivered for Grolier

after years acquired the Triple Crown
for the Southern Methodist Bridwell
the Dove's Press Bible the Kelmscott
Chaucer & Dante of the Ashendene

then arranged for the Harry Ransom
Center acquisitions for untold sums
a Gutenberg & *Gone With the Wind*'s
archive with its antebellum curtains

made into a gown to impress a bank
the Tauchnitz titles Joyce picked up
off railway kiosks to read in Trieste
source for his allusive Homeric text

meantime longed to buy for himself
a high-priced edition of *In Praise of
Folly* where Erasmus says the most
foolish man will weep at the loss of

his mother-in-law to have it he had
to borrow the money as Scarlett did
a young officer hearing 500 dollars
just for a book said they'll laugh me

right out of the business instructed
him in answer to the question he'd
ask A loan for what? should reply
To pay to have the kitchen painted

along with accession of the antique
tomes he'd subsidize art of modern
design of boxes for housing of fine
bookbindings a limited impression

aside from tooled volumes created
& saved he'd adopt & raise Chinese
two together with a son & daughter
take in stray cats feed feral possum

162

from effigies & threats on his life
to rescue Griffin once-blind writer
of *Black Like Me* a '50s Huck Finn
literally saw the light in tinted skin

in the bootblack school of survival
learning pain of a colored entrance
the meaning of Hughes' poetic line
in scattering shadows upset a white

supremacist city council entrusting
manuscripts to this librarian friend
who set him up in an office put him
& the family up in his Dallas home

a wailing wall to John Howard life-
saver who with mud-caked clothes
stripped down before he opened up
& turned any pages in private hands

though herniated would still insist
on lifting cartons in a blizzard ever
generous to a fault not distinguish-
ing Matisse's cut-outs from psalter

appraising equally *Jazz* & hymnal
each work to him in that Maker's
honor never wanted any memorial
said throw a little party & be done

with it or use the celebration fund
for an incunabula a rare blue paper
run with the novelist's inscription
any excuse to build the collection